EARLY CHILDHOOD EDUCATION SERIES
Sharon Ryan, Editor

ADVISORY BOARD: Celia Genishi, Doris Fromberg, Carrie Lobman, Rachel Theilheimer, Dominic Gullo, Amita Gupta, Beatrice Fennimore, Sue Grieshaber, Jackie Marsh, Mindy Blaise, Gail Yuen, Alice Honig, Betty Jones, Stephanie Feeney, Stacie Goffin, Beth Graue

(continued)

BIG SCIENCE
FOR GROWING MINDS

*Constructivist Classrooms
for Young Thinkers*

JACQUELINE GRENNON BROOKS

Foreword by Doris Pronin Fromberg

Teachers College, Columbia University
New York and London

Published by Teachers College Press, 1234 Amsterdam Avenue, New York, NY 10027

Library of Congress Cataloging-in-Publication Data

Brooks, Jacqueline Grennon.
  Big science for growing minds : constructivist classrooms for young thinkers / Jacqueline Grennon Brooks.
    p. cm. — (Early childhood education series)
    Includes bibliographical references and index.
    ISBN 978-0-8077-5195-4 (pbk. : alk. paper)
  1. Science—Study and teaching (Early childhood) I. Title.
  LB1139.5.S35B76 2010
  372.35′044—dc22   2011006670

ISBN 978-0-8077-5195-4 (paper)

Printed on acid-free paper
Manufactured in the United States of America

18 17 16 15 14 13 12 11   8 7 6 5 4 3 2 1

Contents

Foreword

Did you become a teacher in order to emulate the best teachers you had? Did you become a teacher in order to do better than the most rigid teacher you had? When you see brilliant teachers working with young children, you might wonder how they figured out what to do in order to evoke such practice. Professor Jacqueline Grennon Brooks lets us peek inside the process that generates brilliant practice in science education. She connects the learning of science concepts and positive outlooks with specific teaching practice.

Dr. Grennon Brooks speaks directly to the reader with a disarmingly straightforward and personal style. Her voice is profoundly simple, and the book becomes a page turner as it challenges the reader to stump the author with difficult questions. The author anticipates the questions and provides the answers throughout the book in the many vignettes presenting deep analysis of specific topics. The answers are tied up neatly with a ribbon that connects human development, brain research, science standards, integrative learning, and pedagogic strategies. All the while, the content is accessible and sympathetic to the creativity and joy of young learners and their teachers. Jacqueline Grennon Brooks captures the curious child in all of us.

This book answers the important questions of why, what, how, when, and where young children learn and good teachers teach significant science knowledge. The author clearly integrates in caring ways the current concern with assessment and meeting the needs of diverse populations of children.

We need to celebrate the birth of this book. It is a vivid embodiment of how young children learn scientific ideas when their teachers create conditions that match the ways the youngsters are able to integrate meaning. Constructivist practice comes to life in these pages. At a time of narrow high-stakes tests, here is a model that preserves truly professional practice. Congratulations to the author and to Teachers College Press!

—Doris Pronin Fromberg
Hofstra University
January 2011

Acknowledgments

The voices and efforts of many colleagues, friends, students, and children are embedded within these pages, and I value and thank them all. Doris Fromberg, my early childhood education mentor, set the stage for me to write this book. Her ongoing inquiry into the lives of young children is a constant inspiration for my own research, and I see her gracious agreement to write the foreword as the closing of the circle. It was Doris who introduced me to Marie Ellen Lacarda at Teachers College Press, *editor extraordinaire*, who shepherded this project with a firm hand and a gentle touch. She handed the project to Shannon Waite, Nancy Power, Beverly Rivero, and Tania Bissell, each of whom worked with care and collegiality to transform this manuscript into a book that someone might want to read. They each have my respect and appreciation.

I thank Eloise Gmur, Rose Tirotta, and Ana Senra for their precision and, most of all, good spirit in helping to format this book, solve charts and figure out challenges, and check references—not easy tasks.

Nancy Morvillo lent her skillful research talents and keen mind to many of the background science knowledge sections. Stephanie Contreras read the very first versions of this book offering her discerning perspective on what new teachers need in a science education book, and Christine Campisi contributed her insightful classroom reflections to Chapter 5. Vivian Doremus shared her dining room table for a powerful week of perspective-taking.

Lori Antonakakis whipped out not only her camera, but her good nature and creative spirit along with it, and she took the photographs that introduce the lessons of Chapters 12 and 13. Between each and every line of those two chapters are my fond recollections of the endless hours that Cathy Bennett, Tom Mattone, and I spent with thousands of children scrubbing tarnished pennies, cleaning dirty water, making fresh pasta, and wondering what it all meant. Right there beside us were pre-service middle and high school teachers discovering the richness of learning how to teach secondary science from very young scientists. We learned much together.

The children at the Children's Maritime Museum in Port Jefferson, New York, taught me how to set up the cargo challenge of Chapter 5 and the water wheel challenge of Chapter 13 in ways that invite inter-age collaborations. To the children and my colleagues who bring this innovative museum its energy and spirit, thank you for sharing with me the joy of creating something new.

To the many novice and expert teachers and to the children of all ages with whom I have shared many journeys, I say thank you. To my sister Lori Grennon, who read early drafts and helped me clarify and simplify, and to my sister Margery Grennon, who checks out dollar stores with me to find teaching material, I say thank you. To my husband, Martin Brooks, and my children, Emily and Alex Brooks, who help me collect seeds, save string, find rocks, and who still wonder with me about this amazing world we share, I say thank you.

Introduction

The focus of this book is early childhood science education, but the pedagogy, methods, and issues are ageless and inherent in a wide array of subjects. Science occurs in laboratories, concert halls, libraries, kitchens, classrooms, backyards, art galleries, public parks—everyplace. Science is in the mind and we all, regardless of age, take our minds everywhere we go. This book explains science through a set of unifying concepts that serve as the backdrop for science teaching. What are these unifying concepts and where do they come from?

The *Benchmarks for Scientific Literacy* (American Association for the Advancement of Science [AAAS], 2009), first published in 1993, is the popular document that introduced the field's unifying concepts, and the National Science Education Standards (National Research Council, 1996) used them to frame the content standards. In conjunction with many commissions, councils, panels, and committees comprised of thousands of scientists and educators, NSES identifies the unifying concepts as ways to think about the natural and human-made world in terms of relating form and function, examining evolution and equilibrium, making models and offering explanations, measuring, and looking at systems.

On the surface, these concepts may appear remote from early childhood curriculum, but I assert that they have roots in the everyday experiences of all people, young and old, and it is my intention in this book to illustrate that assertion.

I have structured the book around central foundational ideas that address all topics in science, rather than organizing the book into specific science topics, and I have situated educational discussions around a central foundational pedagogy applicable throughout the age span, not one that is unique to early childhood. This organization may seem unusual for an early childhood science book, but I posit that unusual is what we need right now. If we don't rethink early childhood science education, and science education in general, we will never achieve the vision promulgated by NAEYC, NSTA, NRC, NSES, or any of the national commissions that have been studying children and science for so long.

In writing this book, I thought about the definitions of science typically held by my students, who are largely either pre-service or novice teachers. Many of my students come to class thinking science is static and looking for books with fact boxes or lists of important topics to cover. In response, I offer them something different from what they originally seek. If teachers and children engage in the processes of the unifying concepts (relate, look, examine, make, collect, offer, and measure) in the domains cited by the unifying concepts (form, function, equilibrium, evolution, systems, order, organization), children and teachers can generate their own facts from evidence. Facts from evidence typically send learners searching other sources for additional facts. The search for facts unfolds in service of a quest for some overarching concept that helps learners understand more than what they understood before the search.

Most of my students find this new perspective meaningful and even transformative. Most students begin to appreciate the role of wonder and error in their own learning, and they begin to appreciate the merits of evidence-based classroom instruction.

The book is rooted in a constructivist pedagogy that honors the natural scientist within all of us. I have been studying constructivist pedagogy for some years, and as data from the neuroscience community increasingly support the biological underpinnings of constructivism, I remain increasingly committed to it. The neurobiological research is beginning to flourish and provides strong evidence for why the intentional teaching of science is crucial for 3-, 4-, and 5-year-olds.

When students struggle to answer questions that are important to them or spend time solving real-life problems that emerge as relevant, they predictably work hard and want to share their findings. Constructivist teachers prepare classroom settings as safe environments in which students can engage in learning that pushes them beyond the leading edge of their current thinking. They provide the types of tasks that foster student ownership of learning while nurturing their children's abilities to speak, read, write, and listen at increasingly more sophisticated levels. Posing cognitively rich questions, and encouraging students to do the same, creates settings in which content learning, language facility, and creative expression work synergistically.

Constructivist views are commonly misinterpreted as "leave the children alone, don't tell them anything, and see what happens." I aim to dispel that myth and illustrate the deliberate nature of the teacher's role in facilitating the child's interactive, intellectual, and social engagement in academic, scientific studies. Encouraging academic pursuits means building on children's innate curiosity and setting up environments to do it. When teachers can do that with some competence, reason, understanding, and focus, we have stellar science programs at all levels. The book delineates the factors that make up the skill set of teachers who can accomplish this central objective.

Another misconception that I want to make visible and address is the notion that constructivist pedagogy and practices cannot exist in an age of accountability. The flaw in this thinking is that accountability is new. Serious professional educators have always been accountable for the well-being and learning of the children in their classroom. The infusion of standardized testing into preschools, primary schools, and elementary schools may burden the early childhood field with perceived constraints on professional practice, but it doesn't make the field any more accountable. We have always been accountable.

The third misconception that is necessary to dispel is that constructivist classrooms somehow lack the focus and direction necessary to ensure accountability—or, specifically, to prepare children for the standardized tests mentioned previously. Not only is there no evidence to support this notion, but evidence exists to the contrary, as Chapter 2 discusses. The focus and direction of constructivist classrooms provide advantageous rigor through which children develop numerous concepts and skills, some of which are measured on standardized tests.

This book is one that a professor might assign for a college education course, an early childhood or elementary teacher might use as a resource for science curriculum ideas, or a school administrator might distribute to the staff as a starting point to discuss reconceptualizing the pedagogy of their educational programs.

The book is organized into four sections. Part 1, "Science in Early Childhood," presents science as a process of finding out what we don't already know and curriculum as a set of investigations in which children and their teachers can be partners in learning—the children as novice learners and their teachers evolving as master learners. This section frames the pedagogy of the entire book, a constructivist pedagogy contending that we all make our own meaning of the world in which we live.

When teachers provide science lessons as authentic investigations, and not as sets of vocabulary words to be memorized or laws to be repeated, they acknowledge children's roles in developing their own understandings. This section includes the voices of new teachers as they struggle and succeed in offering rich, meaningful science learning opportunities to young children.

Part 2, "Landscapes for Learning Science," opens with a call for teachers to find the curious learner within themselves and ends with examples of how curious learners can make good teachers. The section presents images of classroom explorations based on overarching "big ideas" of science and their role in nurturing children's growth and development. Readers explore ways in which teachers can foster science learning within the classroom, family, community, and nature through active listening, a capacity for ongoing assessment, and an ability to adjust curriculum in response to questions. Readers of this section extend their inquiry into how people learn and question the equity of "equal" learning opportunities.

Part 3, "From Unifying Science Concepts to Curriculum," is a three-chapter sequence in which multiple examples explain the unifying science concepts in ways that make them accessible to early childhood educators. Each time the reader visits a science topic in the book, one or more of the unifying concepts will be explored in the new context of that topic.

Part 4, "From Curriculum to the Wonder of Science," opens with two chapters that describe two integrated, problem-based curriculum units: one unit of chemistry and physics concepts and processes using everyday household items, and one unit of Earth science and biology concepts and processes using water, soil, sand, and salt. This section closes with a discussion of the conditions that must be established in order for successful science teaching and learning to occur on a consistent basis in the classroom. If teachers and children are to be collaborative scientists in the classroom, the classroom environment must be conducive to scientific research.

The science investigations in this book highlight connections among science, mathematics, technology, art, and literacy, and they feature problem-based curricula with multiple solution pathways. The focus of the book is on children's scientific thinking and teachers' pedagogical thinking as children and teachers together strive to build a greater understanding of our beautiful natural and human-made world.

Part 1

SCIENCE IN EARLY CHILDHOOD

CHAPTER 1

Young Scientists with Growing Ideas

The young children we teach have been engaging in the study of science from their earliest days, right alongside their naturally unfolding general growth and development, long before they take their first steps into a school.

CHILDREN GROW UP BY GROWING IDEAS

Four-year-old Alex has been gathering "scientific data" for 4 years. As a baby, he made sense of his world by using his senses—watching, listening, talking, smelling, and touching—as much as he could. He collected data using his senses and made meaning from his data by building connections among actions and reactions. These connections multiplied as he personally researched his unfolding world. Maybe he mentally concluded: "If I whimper slightly, I am fed." Or maybe his data pointed to the conclusion "I have to scream pretty long and hard before I am fed." At different moments, he may have built the connection "When something good happens, I smile, and then good things happen again!" Or maybe he found that "When something good happens, I smile, and I smile alone."

Baby Alex grew to combine his senses. As a toddler, he watched what he touched and talked about what he smelled. He asked questions and insisted on answers. When not satisfied with the answers, he insisted on better ones—that is, answers that made sense to him.

For a long time before coming to school, Alex expressed keen interest in studies of cause and effect: What happens if I drop this spoon? What happens if I grab that child's toy? What if I keep stacking the blocks after she says to clean up? What happens if I pour three cups of sand instead of the two cups I mixed last time? Alex, like all children, will be a natural scientist his whole life, unless someone or some event stamps it out of him.

What Alex learned from his first years of explorations differs from what Anna learned. Alex's parents returned dropped spoons. Anna's parents sighed and told her to pay attention to what she was doing. If the spoon was filled with ice cream and landed on a rug or spattered on a shirt or a wall, Alex's parents cleaned up the mess with a reassurance that it is okay to make mistakes. In contrast, Anna's parents just sighed. Anna's caregiver, on the other hand, thinks that building the tallest tower possible and watching it fall to pieces is a fun afternoon event. But Alex's caregiver doesn't want to see any strewn toys or hear noises. Sometimes both Anna and Alex get confused by how grown-ups behave, and sometimes the grown-ups cannot figure out Anna's or Alex's behavior.

Let's meet 4-year-old Maya. Maya downloads software that turns her computer into an alarm clock. She specifies the sound file to be played and wakes up to her favorite song. After breakfast, she puts on the earplugs from her iPod, places her cell phone in her pocket, deposits her personal digital assistant (PDA) into her backpack, and is ready for school. In her young life, Maya takes care of virtual pets on tiny screens and has a phone that announces the callers, clocks that announce the time, and lights that flick on when she speaks.

The tools, relationships, types of human contact, and amenities in all children's lives create the unique environments in which they live. And these environments, whether they are either filled with or devoid of opportunity, are physically changing their brains.

CHILDREN GROW SMART BY GROWING IDEAS

We have all long wondered about the specific links between the functioning of the brain and a child's behavior and thoughts. We have also long witnessed children's behavior and the evidence of their thinking through what they produce—stories they tell, pictures they draw, ideas they share, and responses they give to test questions, informal or formal, among other glimpses into their inner worlds.

While neuroscience is still in its infancy when compared to other branches of scientific research, the field has produced over the last 2 decades—and continues to produce at unprecedented rates—new information about the brain and the two-way street between brain and behavior. The brain affects behavior, and behavior affects the brain. The brain changes in response to experience. We call the brain's malleability, or its ability to reorganize its own neural pathways, *neuroplasticity*. Neuroplasticity refers to the imprints of experience that last as the anatomical and physiological features of the brain (Nelson and Luciana, 2001; Shreeve, 2005; Tortora & Grabowski, 1996).

In a simplified summary of brain activity, we can say that the brain makes cells, grows the structures of the cell necessary to send and receive messages, strengthens or prunes those structures as experience dictates, and insulates the structures so that the messages are sent efficiently and quickly. The explosion of neural connections, called "exuberant" by neuroscientists, indicates that the young human brain prepares to process all types of experiences. Then, through the early years, neural pathways that are exercised become stronger and larger, developing more connections; those that are not used die. Together, proliferation and pruning enhance the efficiency of neural communication while simplifying the brain's overall organization. (Huttenlocher, 2002).

Although, as an organ, the human brain has not evolved significantly over the last 40,000 years, Siegel (2010) posits that today's brain would reveal an enormously more intricate network of neural structures than would a 40,000-year-old brain: "The mind uses the brain to create itself" (Siegel, 2010, p. 261).

Most of the research on how experience affects the developing brain has involved harmful events, such as neglect, stress, or impairment. The studies that explore the relationship between enriched environments and brain development have been conducted on animals. However, as Shonkoff and Phillips (2000) state, "Moving from these animal studies to research on the neurological aspects of human cognitive, linguistic, and social-emotional development is a big leap, but one that warrants a major investment of time and resources" (p. 198).

Although researchers are cautious about linking any specific form of an enriched physical environment for young children with any specific type of physical brain development, the past decade has witnessed the rise of educational programs that are based on inferences from research and marketed as brain based (Krakovsky, 2005). Even under the umbrella of caution, there are reasonable approaches to designing early childhood programs aligned with both neuroscientific research and behavioral development research. The Institute for Early Childhood Education puts forth two implications from the field of neuroscience that are supported by behavioral research:

> The experiences that are developmentally provocative will change as the brain matures; . . . and interaction with appropriately responsive social partners is one of the most developmentally provocative experiences for the growing brain. (Thompson, 2008, p. 6)

Anatomical changes in the brain have dramatic effects because they influence future learning. In turn, learning and a child's total welfare and development are significantly influenced by early experiences (Gopnic, Meltzoff, & Kuhl, 1999).

Figure 1.1 speaks loudly and seriously to early childhood educators. The dark grey line of the graph indicates that neural activity for higher

FIGURE 1.1. Brain development for different functions at different ages (Source: Shonkoff et al., & Phillips, 2000).

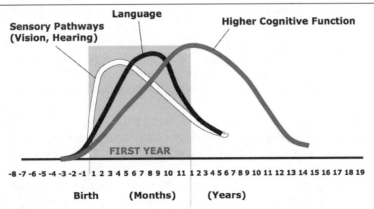

cognitive functioning is at a peak during the preschool and kindergarten years. Science investigations prompt the precise mental activities defined as higher cognitive functioning. Thus, while science education can and does occur throughout life, science education in preschool and kindergarten is every child's right and every educator's responsibility.

Since the neurons of the brain change as a result of experience, the case for healthy, intellectually rich learning environments for young children is now supported by neuroscientists in addition to educators and parents! Yoon and Onchwari (2006) state that "[S]tudies emphasize developing effective early childhood education programs because 'rich' experiences produce rich brains" (p. 416). These ideas are revisited in Chapter 6, "Science of Learning."

Emerging data suggest a link between brain development and the type of education within constructivist classrooms (Michaels, Shouse, & Schweingruber, 2007).

CONSTRUCTIVIST CLASSROOMS

As Fensham states, "The most conspicuous psychological influence on curriculum thinking in science since 1980 has been the constructivist view of learning" (1992, p. 801). This view sees learners of all ages as inferring meaning from noticeable events and building knowledge by organizing these inferences. Constructivist classrooms provide diverse opportunities for learners to construct meaning in various contexts with multiple objects, people, things, and ideas. Throughout this book, children's learning and teacher practice are described using a constructivist lens.

Constructivist teaching principles emerge from constructivist theories of learning. These principles explain how teachers can teach in ways that keep the power of learning within children while exercising authority as classroom leaders.

Let's return to Alex, Anna, and Maya and meet their kindergarten teacher, Ms. Connolly. Ms. Connolly wants to welcome her students to a classroom that can contribute to the science learning that the children began at home. Here are the four principles upon which this book is based, and upon which Ms. Connolly bases her teaching practice (Brooks & Brooks, 1999; Brooks, 2002):

- value students' points of view,
- structure lessons around big ideas,
- pose problems of emerging relevance, and
- tie teaching to assessment during the process of teaching.

The first principle that guides Ms. Connolly's professional decision-making is to value students' points of view. She views Anna, Alex, and Maya as complex, critical, and creative thinkers. She knows that however young they may be, they have already begun studying the changing and diverse worlds in which they live and have already constructed many ideas about how their worlds work. Ms. Connolly looks to understand each child's presently constructed ideas by asking herself questions.

As babies, what did Alex, Anna, and Maya learn from flinging spoons? As toddlers, what meaning did they make from playing with other children's toys? In preschool, what did the children find out about ignoring calls to clean up? Now, in kindergarten, what do they infer about making mistakes? As 1st or 2nd graders proposing one experiment after the other, what might Maya, Alex, and Anna learn about initiation and curiosity?

Ms. Connolly honors the perspective of each child and tries to understand each child's ways of making sense out of experience. She stays ready to embark with the children on the next steps of their science journeys. Together, they venture into new topics, expand thoughts that have already begun, and refine present understandings. Chapter 2 describes Ms. Connolly's class with specific science lesson examples.

PROFESSIONAL KNOWLEDGE STANDARDS

The National Association for the Education of Young Children (NAEYC) offers a set of standards that delineate a teacher's professional knowledge base. This book spirals through all of the NAEYC standards throughout the volume but highlights a specific standard in each chapter. In this chapter, we highlight the Promoting Child Development and Learning standard (NAEYC, 2009).

Promoting Child Development and Learning

Candidates use their understanding of young children's characteristics and needs, and of multiple interacting influences on children's development and learning, to create environments that are healthy, respectful, supportive, and challenging for all children.

Teachers need a palette of professional actions in order to create environments that are healthy, respectful, supportive, and challenging for all children. A full palette is necessary because at all moments during the day, teachers use context-appropriate strategies that are appropriate to the learning situation. A teacher needs diagnostic skills in order to offer curriculum that is well matched to the leading edge of young children's current thinking. For example, sometimes teachers can enhance learning by helping children *expand* their thinking in a particular direction. At other times, teachers can enhance learning by helping children *limit* their thinking to a specific observation. On other occasions, teachers can enhance learning by *redirecting* children's perspectives to a domain of her initiation.

The examples in the upcoming chapters of this book illustrate curriculum and instructional strategies that seek to meet children where they are and support them in going as far as they can go.

TECHNOLOGY FOR YOUNG CITIZENS

In today's world, meeting and supporting students requires an understanding of technology. It is everywhere. Regardless of how many or what type of electronics each child in each family has, teachers need to understand how the world of electronics is affecting all of us and when and how to use the electronic world in service of young children's growth and development.

The world of technology is dramatically changing science from how we collect and store data to how we analyze and distribute data (Trefil, 2008). Technology is dramatically increasing the need for citizens to understand science in order to participate in debate about the critical issues that are emerging from the use of technology (Sagan, 1995) and the energy those technologies use. We have washing machines that tell us how they plan to clean the clothes, ovens that turn off when they determine the meal is ready to eat, and vacuum cleaners that light up when they determine the rug is clean enough. All of these devices save time, make us feel safer, entertain us, and keep us clean or fed. But not all of us. These amenities are economically and culturally dependent, reflecting a host of societal inequalities that leave their imprint on the brain.

In today's schools, even in localities in which the children live in families of modest or little wealth, technology is everywhere. Smart boards—with which the teachers and children can access the Internet; call up previously stored animations, photos, or texts; or use a seemingly endless supply of shapes, charts, diagrams, or maps—roll around the school on wheels or are mounted in the classrooms. LED (light emitting diode) displays light up cafeterias; plasma TVs can be found in school libraries and classrooms; and a host of other devices, all with on and off switches, are scattered throughout the school.

The downside of these electronic technologies from a learning perspective is that the devices are "black boxes," a term used in science to refer to any object with hidden inner workings. In today's wireless world, even the "objects" themselves are hidden. We instantly message a friend on the other side of the world. How many people can explain that black box? How does Ms. Connolly help her students understand what is happening behind the buttons, trackballs, and touch pads? What are the pathways between children's present functioning and their eventual understanding of electronic systems that are such a part of our daily lives?

THE IMPORTANCE OF SIMPLE

One strategy Ms. Connolly uses is to purposively seek out the simpler objects and substances that predate the conveniences that are common within today's world. Is she saying that the leading edge of education is in the past? No. She is saying that offering children opportunities to "reinvent the wheel" is important. Understanding the processes that lead to outcomes that are part of their everyday lives, but that are typically hidden from view or experience, help us to look forward.

Asking simple questions about our world is imperative to understanding it. Many children enjoy a sprinkle of parmesan on their spaghetti. How is cheese grated? Lentil soup sounds tasty. How long does it take to make hard beans soft? How do you mix flour and water and what do you get when you mix them? What about shaking cream in a jar? Or mixing colors in cups of water? Or mixing colors in hot and cold water? And the list continues. Young children need multiple chances in various domains to understand the mechanics that produce the common foods and goods of our world. The important learning question is: How do objects and substances interact?

Children in Ms. Connolly's class might learn how the dry pasta in the cardboard boxes got there by participating in the many steps it takes to make their own pasta, dry it, and package it. They may learn how to get the water out of fruit and how to get it back in. They engage in a number of investigations that help them peek into processes that they rarely see happen. Unlike with making pasta, however, Ms. Connolly's children cannot likely investigate how the many electronic devices they use work. But they can begin an intellectual journey toward understanding the mechanics that predate the electronics. The science of copying images provides an example.

Carbon paper is almost an antique in today's world! But in using it, the writer can see the new copy emerging from the pressure of her own hand. Anna, Alex, and Maya can see an action and a consequence beyond the button-pushing on a copy machine. Pressure-sensitive paper, although more mysterious than carbon paper, still allows them to see the outcomes of actions as they unfold. These are old technologies, but they provide possible learning prospects for Maya, Anna, and Alex that electronic copiers can't provide.

Young children need three-dimensional opportunities for exploration and from which young children can construct fundamental knowledge. Just like adults, young children seek needed information very often through tools, whether the tool is a simple device such as a pencil or a sophisticated device such as a computer.

We live, work, and play on a new landscape formed in large part by an electronic, wireless, World Wide Web of instant communication, a landscape that is changing even as you read this book. Thus, the landscape of learning is also sculpted by this rapidly evolving complex system of technologies and the many people who design and use them, then redesign and reuse them. Technology has always played a big role in science, and science has always played a big role in technology. They can be important parts of learning settings, but teachers need to analyze their use carefully (Linn, Davis and Bell, 2004).

The message for teachers in this new time of burgeoning technology is to remember the importance of simple technologies for young children. These simple technologies can provide a mental foundation upon which a child can build links among phenomena and generate bigger, more generalized, more inclusive ideas known as unifying concepts. The notion of unifying concepts is discussed in depth in Chapter 9.

Primary education can start children on journeys that invite them to question how their worlds work and prompt them to design better ways to work within them.

SPACES FOR GROWING IDEAS

Friedrich Froebel, the 18th-century educator, who is considered to be the founder of the kindergarten movement, originally envisioned the early childhood classroom as a learning space for the cultivation of new ideas, self-generated investigations, and interdisciplinary study (Lilley, 2010). Since those days in the 1800s, young children have had access to enormously increasing sources of information. Yet the developmental patterns of young children have not changed dramatically.

We are living in a period of significant transitions. The technological world is changing how we interact and the speed of our interactions, and the neurobiological world is changing how we understand our interactions. Within and among all of these new opportunities and challenges, we can and must create spaces for science learning, spaces where ideas sprout and grow and spaces where children can discover the beauty of science. But in order for teachers to create spaces to learn about the beauty of our world, teachers need to see it as beautiful. Famed physicist Richard Feynman opens *The National Science Education Standards* (National Research Council, 1996) document with the following quote:

> The world looks so different after learning science. For example, trees are made of air, primarily. When they are burned, they go back to air, and in the flaming heat is released the flaming heat of the sun which was bound in to convert the air into tree. And in the ash is the small remnant of the part which did not come from air, [which] came from the solid earth, instead. These are beautiful things. (p. 1)

The National Science Education Standards call for a new direction in science education, one in which teachers engage children in investigations that enhance emerging competence in content learning and processing skills, a competence that enhances the likelihood that children will see the beauty that Mr. Feynman sees.

NATIONAL SCIENCE EDUCATION STANDARDS

Understanding big ideas of science is an important piece of the necessary professional knowledge that teachers of young children need. Thus, in addition to the NAEYC professional standards that guide teachers in fostering young children's thinking and development, this book also describes the National Science Education Standards. With both sets of standards, educators can create preschools, kindergartens, and primary schools for young children that are intentionally designed spaces for growing science ideas.

In its study of instructional practices, the National Research Council (NRC), a primary authoring organization of the National Science Education Standards (NSES), found that early childhood science programs were typically offering 20-minute lessons in which children were engaging in activities such as naming parts of a flower or identifying an animal and its baby. Investigations were found to be infrequent, but when they occurred, much teacher time was spent managing the materials and children's movements. Rarely did teachers ask young children to explain their thinking or give reasons for conclusions. Teachers rarely allowed or encouraged children to investigate questions that interested them or to design their own experiments. Lessons often focused on following direction and memorizing names rather than investigating interesting questions.

The results from classrooms that engage children with short, prescribed activities to answer a question the teacher poses have been disappointing in two ways: there is minimal evidence that learners use what they have learned in science classes in new domains; and the minimal numbers of life-long science learners (Linn et al., 2004). Thus, the Science Standards include a large section on "changing emphases" (see Figure 1.2).

In order to improve science learning, the Science Standards provide a new emphasis on integrating a child's science investigation with her ability to articulate and communicate her ideas; work productively with others to craft plans and arguments; and in short, use the classroom as a research laboratory with social, affective, mathematical, literary, and scientific components. The recommendations of the Science Standards for science education programs put children's natural curiosity and investigation at the core.

Studying a few fundamental science concepts through a process over which the young child has design control is the hallmark of the changing emphases of learning science content and is far more meaningful than "covering" a large number of concepts—less is more. But the Science Standards do not suggest that teachers teach children less. On the contrary: Children learn more when teachers "cover" *less* information and create more opportunity to construct knowledge together.

Although information and knowledge are used interchangeably in common conversation and are considered synonyms by some, they have very different meanings in the field of education and it is imperative for a teacher to distinguish the differences. The first thing that teachers need to know about information is that it is not knowledge. Information consists of the facts we collect, whereas knowledge is the sense we make from putting lots of facts together.

The Science Standards stress the importance of the sense-making process and the challenge-based context in which learning occurs. As the authenticity of the challenge increases, so does the willingness of children to engage in the knowledge construction necessary to address the challenge. Children

FIGURE 1.2. Changing emphases in instructional strategies.

FROM		TO
Verifying science concept	→	Investigating science question
Short investigations	→	Long investigations
Get an answer	→	Explain using evidence
Science as exploration	→	Science as argument
Answer questions	→	Communicate explanations

in settings that encourage investigation actually seek out information that will help them solve the challenges before them. A teacher who can guide a young child's thinking and activities along this line is the teacher every child needs.

A SIMPLE MESSAGE

Teaching young children science sets a stage on which much future learning in all subject areas can unfold. This is why it is so important for pre-K and kindergarten teachers, as well as parents and caregivers, to build a platform strong enough to hold the weighty ideas that children grow all day, all night, and all year. Learning science is an exciting, important, and necessary enterprise for young children.

All adults, with intention or not, are science teachers of young children. This volume refers to all adults who interact with children as "teachers," all inquiries as "lessons," and every place in which learning can occur as a "classroom."

The book proceeds with a simple message—explore with the young people in your life the splendid surprises new days bring, and you'll be both a science *learner* and a science *teacher*!

Chapter 2

A Constructivist View of Learning

Constructivism enjoys a long and rich history in the fields of psychology, epistemology, and philosophy. As Figure 2.1 illustrates, constructivism is a learning theory that includes discussions of important issues relating to the study of the mind, the study of knowledge, and the study of "reality."

Constructivism is based on the notion that learners generate meaning though mental formulation and reformulation of concepts that satisfy a search for understanding. The theory is often associated with the well-known psychologist Jean Piaget, who contributed immensely to our understandings of young children's development. However, historians credit 18th-century philosopher Giambattista Vico with the first use of "constructivism" to describe the notion that people can know only what their cognitive structures, shaped by experience, allow them to know (von Glaserfeld, 1995).

In his early career, Piaget scored and analyzed tests for the famous psychometrician Alfred Binet. In so doing, Piaget discovered that there were

FIGURE 2.1. Constructivist learning theory.

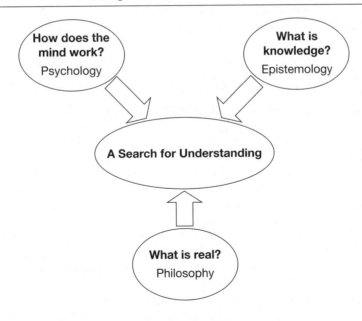

some multiple-choice questions that high percentages of young children always got wrong. But he also discovered an interesting phenomenon: On some questions, nearly 80% of young children selected the same "wrong" answer. This was perplexing to him. He reasoned that, if students did not know the "right" answer to the questions, and were simply guessing, one would expect a reasonably close distribution among the four answer choices (about 25% for each choice). He concluded that the children were not really guessing. For young children of specific ages, the "wrong" answer was actually their perceived "right" answer. This tweaked Piaget's interest in child development and led him to a lifelong study of it.

Constructivism has a relatively short and controversial history in the field of education. The following quote reveals that the nature of science appears to be at the heart of the controversy, along with related questions about what is "true."

> There is a not-too-subtle difference between the constructivist formulation "making sense," and the realist formulation "finding out." The former has no epistemological or referential bite; the latter has both. Things can make perfect sense without being true; and making still more sense does not imply any increase in truth content. (Matthews, 1998, p. 5)

This book presents the terms "making sense" and "finding out" as being more related to each other than Matthews (1998) suggests in the above quote. Children engage in a process of *making sense* of the happenings around them in order to *find out* about how their world works. Teaching young children science means the teacher is an ambassador of today's conventionally accepted scientific content, with just enough intellectual skepticism to keep everyone open to novel perspectives.

While, as Matthews states, things can make sense without being true, it can also be stated that unless the truth makes sense to a child, the child has no way to use that truth. Unless a child puts pieces of information together so that an idea makes sense, that idea, whether considered true by adults or not, will likely not be true to the child. Inert truths are simply not valuable.

To accept a child's "sense making" tied to knowingly false premises and letting the teaching opportunity slide by would be irresponsible. For example, let's look at a lesson in Ms. Connolly's class in which a group of children come across a cartoon in which the three characters are trying to decide whether or not to put a coat on a snowman to "keep him cold" and stop him from melting. See Figure 2.2 (this illustration can be found at http://www.conceptcartoons.com/science/subway—1.htm).

The children used what they knew about putting on their own coat in the winter to keep warm and applied it to the snowman problem. These children concluded that a coat would help to keep the snowman cold.

Ms. Connolly used the opportunity to pull out some different fabrics, some thermometers, and some ice and asked the children to see what happens to the "iceman." She gathered materials analogous to what is suggested in the cartoon and wondered aloud what might happen with the ice if she put a coat on it. What happens to a snowman with or without a coat depends on many factors and cannot be answered with a simple "It will melt faster" or "It will melt slower" answer. But, in changing the problem to

FIGURE 2.2. Snowman problem (Source: Naylor, S., & Keogh, B., 2000).

one that could be answered through activity on real objects, Ms. Connolly set the stage for "sense making" tied to evidence. This is real science. This is learning science through doing science.

The following four principles can guide teachers in working with children and form the basis for the curriculum and instructional approaches throughout this book.

BUILDING BIG IDEAS

The first teaching principle for teachers to consider when preparing a lesson is to structure the lessons around a big idea. Big ideas are the foundational concepts on which other concepts are built. Children need to construct big ideas in many domains and in many contexts by investigating data, scenarios, phenomena, or events in ways that help them see patterns. Seeing patterns leads to forging and understanding big ideas.

What are big ideas? Here is one in simple language: "Forces cannot be seen, but we can see what happens when they are around." In child-friendly language, we call forces "pushes" and "pulls." Think of the following lesson that invites young children to investigate this big idea about forces.

The Right Materials

Ms. Connolly can engage her children in an investigation of forces, or pushes and pulls, using a range of materials. But after overhearing a few children talking about how much they love bubbles, she decides to capitalize on their current interest in bubbles and chooses that material for lessons on forces. She sets forth the challenge: "Try to keep the bubbles floating in the air for as long as possible."

The children intuitively start blowing their breath or waving their hands under the bubbles. Sometime it seems to work, but most times it doesn't. By happenstance, Cameron gets Kelly's bubble to swing over to his side and somehow hover. Cameron's hands are above the bubble and he quite excitedly keeps up the waving and the bubble lasts a bit longer, but is still in place. By now, many children are excited and try this new technique with much success.

The Right Questions

The question of why emerges quite quickly because waving your hands over the bubble is counterintuitive when trying to keep it aloft. At this point, Ms. Connolly very much influences how much learning can take place. Based on her observations of student engagement and hearing student statements about the outcomes of waving their hands, she decides that her original idea of using bubbles to investigate pushes and pulls was heading in a reasonable direction, and she poses questions such as "What do you notice about how close the bubble is to your hand?" The children generate the following observations:

"The bubble goes near my hand."
"If we wave on top of the bubble, the bubble goes up."
"If we wave below the bubble, it goes down."
"There is something special about waving."

Ms. Connolly asks, "Does waving our hands always pull the bubble toward our hands?" No one answers the question, but Jamie suggests that everyone wave together over one bubble, and the whole class likes the idea. In doing so, Joseph remarks that they are "like a fan." Mary has a hand fan at home that she got as a present and wants to bring it in to try. Mary's offer reminds Joseph that he, too, has a fan at home—one "that you plug in"—and he wants to bring it to school, too. Teri knows that there is a fan in the janitor's room and asks if she can borrow it. Jaime offers to bring in her mom's hair dryer, saying that it is "stronger than a fan."

The children are intellectually sparking each other's ideas and Ms. Connolly encourages the discourse and brainstorming.

The Right Science

Ms. Connolly knows that the scientific principle explaining why waving a hand above a bubble to keep the bubble aloft is a sophisticated concept, too advanced for virtually all preschoolers and kindergartners. In fact, the principle is counterintuitive for almost everyone, of any age.

As you increase the speed of air by waving your hand (you may never have thought about it or may never have recognized it), you have actually produced a region of lower air pressure. Air moves from high to low pressure, tending toward equilibrium. As the air moves from the region of higher pressure to the region of lower pressure, it brings the bubble with it, in this case upward. It's quite a surprise to most people.

Thinking about the phenomenon further, you may remember the pull of your car when you are stopped at a red light waiting to turn, while the ongoing traffic whizzes by. Or you may remember the feel of a shower curtain brushing inward against your body after you have turned on the fast-streaming shower. Think about other examples. What about those magnificent birds in the sky? Are their movements in the sky related to the children's hand-waving near the bubbles? Yes, it is.

So what does Ms. Connolly do right now? In what direction can the lesson proceed so as to engage children in an investigation that is developmentally sound for their present thinking?

Ms. Connolly knows that there is a developmentally sound and scientifically accurate version of the sophisticated principle that sets the stage for future thinking and investigation. This version also keeps curiosity alive. She knows that this phenomenon can be investigated using many different common objects, and, during the course of a child's study in her class and in the school, the children, indeed, have opportunities to investigate this phenomenon in different contexts.

For example, placing a Ping-Pong ball over a hair dryer and letting go of the ball will result in its suspension—another surprise for most people! The fast-moving air below the Ping-Pong ball causes an area of low pressure. The slower moving air above the ball rushes around to equalize the pressure, thus causing the Ping-Pong ball to spin in place with apparently nothing holding it up or preventing it from shooting away—except air pressure!

Although the concepts of air pressure are beyond the comprehension of those in their early childhood years, the ability to see the evidence of air pressure is not. In another example, blowing hard through the space between two pieces of paper held in your hands will move the papers toward each other. Again, the result is quite a surprise to most! The reason is the same: the fast-moving air as a result of blowing creates an area of low pressure between the pieces of paper.

The same phenomenon occurs by blowing hard through the space between two balls suspended by strings: The balls move toward each other. Again, it is counterintuitive, but true. The objects are different, but the result is the same: The balls move toward the fast-moving air. These are two more examples, among many.

Without going any further with the investigation, there is already a very big content idea that Ms. Connolly and her children addressed within the context of this one lesson: Pushes and pulls cannot be seen, but we can see what happens when they are around. A big social/emotional idea is "I know *what* happens, and I know it has something to do with pushes and pulls, but I do not yet know *why* it happens." These are two big ideas that are ready for modification and ready for transferability if and when another learning context emerges.

In the meantime, the content learning that "pushes and pulls cannot be seen, but we can see what happens when they are around" is a huge physical science idea on which much of the study of physics rests. It is important to stress that the teacher must refrain from "giving away answers." Giving away vocabulary words as "answers" to problems is not good science teaching. Aiming children toward setting up solvable problems is.

Let's continue looking at Ms. Connolly's class, but now from another perspective—that of how a teacher poses problems that develop during ongoing exploration, problems that we refer to as those with emerging relevance.

PROBLEMS OF EMERGING RELEVANCE

The second teaching principle teachers keep in mind after determining the big idea or big ideas of upcoming lessons is to determine a problem with potential relevance for children. A few pieces of information and a good question help young children become both curious and uncertain at the same time, and these lesson components open children up to the surprise of new insights. An example appears in the section below.

Saying, Seeing, Controlling, and Explaining

The challenge in Ms. Connolly's class is, How can we keep the bubbles floating in the air for as long as possible? This challenge serves to encourage children to search for patterns within and linkages to what they already know about bubbles. Ms. Connolly asks, "What do you notice about how close the bubble is to your hand?" Dependent on what she sees happening with the children and what she hears them say, she could also ask, Does how fast you wave your hand matter? Does it matter if two people wave their hands together? These are just two questions of many that she can pose.

The "good question" in this lesson is really not a question. Rather, it is a challenge: "Try to keep the bubbles floating in the air for as long as possible." As the investigation continues, Ms. Connolly changes the challenge to the following: "Try to keep the bubbles aloft as long as possible." Note also the use of the word "aloft." Ms. Connolly repeats the challenge using the word "aloft" after having repeatedly used the term "keeping the bubble floating in the air."

The natural use of leading-edge vocabulary by the teacher is another aspect of posing problems of emerging relevance. Vocabulary also emerges with kinesthetic and language experiences. The children are saying "aloft," seeing aloft, controlling aloft, and explaining aloft.

The above scenario in Ms. Connolly's class illustrates a quick emergence of the problem's relevance. However, we see relevance emerge in lessons in which the materials and the questions are not as initially significant to young children as in the case of bubbles.

Preparing for Problems

On another day, Ms. Connolly's class was using sieves and strainers with different-size holes to see which order works best to get the greatest number of piles of different-sized rocks. It is likely that none of the children woke up that morning wondering about rocks and the size of holes through which they could pass. But the problem emerged as relevant in the context of making and thinking about piles of rocks. Relevance is not under the control of the teacher. It resides within each student. The teacher's role is to provide interesting enough information, and a good enough question. In Ms. Connolly's class, we see a teacher teaching within an intentionally emerging curriculum. She negotiates the curriculum with the children. It originates and unfolds in interactions among children, and Ms. Connolly intentionally designs frameworks in which and through which the children can safely and energetically engage with ideas.

The big ideas of science in which Ms. Connolly's children are engaged can be explored with both younger and older children. Big science ideas are everywhere all the time, as are science "problems" to solve. It is the skillful teacher who can find the intellectually challenging point for children of different ages, dispositions, and prior experience. That skillfulness develops from constantly refreshing one's own knowledge base with the science concepts (the big ideas), designing interesting problems for children to solve (problems of emerging relevance) and, next, valuing children's perspectives.

POINTS OF VIEW

The third teaching principle is for teachers to value students' points of view. Valuing students' ideas and points of view sounds simple. But how easy is it to really understand someone else's point of view? Experienced teachers find that it is not as easy as it may appear. For young children, the capacity to understand the viewpoints of others is only beginning to develop between the ages of 2 and 4. For adults, it takes constant observation and self-reflection to develop the capacity within.

In order to enhance our valuing of students' viewpoints, let's engage in the following exercise. Look at the two slides in Figure 2.3. What story do they tell you?

FIGURE 2.3. A "simple" story (Credit: Jamie Charteris, © 2000).

People of all ages see different stories. They bring different value systems, different experiences, and different projections onto these two simple pictures. Who is the mother? Who is the teacher? Is the child happy at school or not? What does the mother "really" look like? People hold very strong views about these questions after only having seen the pictures for a short time.

Valuing students' points of view requires considerable thinking and reserved judgment on the part of the teacher. The teacher wants to invite participation long enough so that divergent views can emerge. If divergent views are not suggested by the children, the teacher can provoke new lines of thinking with questions, such as, "Does everyone think this person is the mother?" "Could she be the teacher?"

Many teachers wonder how they could honor children's thinking and still cover the curriculum. Honoring a child's perspective seems outside of the curriculum if a teacher has not envisioned the curriculum through children's eyes. Most of what children think is tied to, or can be tied to, the curriculum. A child's comment during a lesson is typically inspired, in some fashion, by some element of the lesson. The teacher weaves classroom comments together, creating important discussion in the classroom.

Discussion Versus Conversation

How does classroom discussion differ from casual conversation? Discussion builds connections among ideas that come from the children (Forman & Fyfe, 1998). It refers to a formal time in the classroom when the teacher is evoking student responses as the mechanism to focus children's attentions in a particular direction.

Consider Ms. Connolly's lesson on rocks. Ms. Connolly begins with a plan to focus Jane and Tatiana's attention on the ordering of the different sieves based on the size of the holes in the sieve screens:

> *Jane*: I saw that I needed to use the sieves with big holes first, then use the sieves with littler holes.
> *Tatiana*: I have a really big rock in my backyard.
> *Ms. Connolly*: We're hearing Tatania tell us that there's a really big rock in her backyard. How big would the holes have to be to catch that rock in a sieve? Tatania, please show us with your hands how big the rock is?

To some teachers Tatania's comment was tangential. But Ms. Connolly found a way to incorporate Tatania's comment into the purpose of the lesson, which was to develop relationships between two sets of objects—sieves and rocks—and create two ordered series of sieves and rocks.

Connecting to the Curriculum

Let's return to Ms. Connolly's bubble lessons to help us understand how a teacher can value young children's points of view and still "stick with" the curriculum. The idea of a 5-year-old child borrowing a fan from the janitor, within a lesson using bubbles to study forces, may seem "outside the curriculum," an example of getting off topic and not covering the curriculum. But in this lesson, the fan had everything to do with the curriculum. In fact, many would say that it went "through and beyond" the curriculum.

Within the lesson time, Ms. Connolly tied the fan to forces by highlighting the observation that the bubbles went even faster toward the fan than toward the children's waving hands. She turned the children's attention to unifying concepts. There is an *order* in observing the fact that the fan is more powerful than the hand. The blades of the fan move faster than the hand.

There is an *organization* emerging: The fan and the waving hands work in similar ways.

- The hand can *model* the fan.
- The fan can *model* the hand.
- There are many more possible connections.

The teacher does not have to highlight all of the connections. Rather, he or she needs to be aware of them and then choose which to highlight as appropriate opportunities arise.

All young children come to every experience with their own points of view, their own ideas about how their worlds work. When adults assume that virtually all of the students think alike, and then structure lessons around only one way of thinking, they too often miss opportunities for large numbers of students to make connections.

Young children may approach learning situations with similar mental structures and cognitive skills, but given divergent cultural and family backgrounds, they do not all think alike, and the only way adults come to know what they are thinking is by seeking and valuing children's unique points of view. When children have opportunities to talk about and act out their ideas with materials, adults can begin to see what children know and how they perceive different problems and situations.

It is interesting to note that most children's ideas within a particular topic coalesce around a few big conceptions, accurate or not. Sometimes, children have the same right idea, and sometimes they have the same wrong idea. But unless the teacher finds out, the chance that the lesson will result in learning is compromised.

TIE TEACHING TO ASSESSMENT

The fourth principle teachers need to keep in mind is that of tying teaching to authentic instruction-based assessments of children's thinking. Good instruction puts children's performance at the center of the classroom for two reasons. Children's performance provides a pre-test for next teaching steps and it provides a post-test of what has been learned to date.

The simplest sounding questions can serve as both pre-assessment and post-assessment instruments: What happens to this tea bag in cold water?

How can we clean this dirty water? Let's see what happens to this ice on these different materials. Any hunches? With these questions as prompts, children design ways to find out what happens, and their activities provide teachers with opportunities to determine what has been learned thus far and how to proceed in upcoming lessons.

Notice that the pre-assessment and post-assessment questions look very much like the problems of emerging relevance described as teaching principle #2. They are the same because it is more useful to think about assessment as lessons rather than instruments.

Pre-assessment/Post-assessment Lessons

On an ongoing basis, teachers adapt lesson plans to the specific children in the class, differentiating the lessons to respond to what the teachers analyzed as a need through the pre-assessment lessons. Thus, tying teaching to assessment also implies tying assessment to teaching—it forms a cycle. One informs the other and sets the stage for the next. Therefore, with this frame of mind, reading a book or watching a phenomenon unfold and asking the children to share their favorite part may be a fine activity for a number of reasons, but it does not serve as a useful assessment of learning of big science ideas for next step teaching.

Listen for Learning

Ms. Connolly's class provides an example of how a teacher listens for learning and interprets what she hears to determine next teaching steps. Hearing and seeing Mary's offer to bring in a fan or Jaime's offer of a hair dryer is an insight into those children's ways of thinking. The offers carry much information, if a teacher knows what to look for. What do these offers tell Ms. Connolly about these children's categorical and relational thinking? They serve as a clue to the children's abilities to see relationships based on certain functions—ways to make air move faster. The children's abilities to explain why a fan or a blow dryer would be a good item to use in the floating bubble investigation is a clue to their representational thinking—how they communicate their ideas.

Ms. Connolly assesses the learners in order to formulate a follow-up lesson that can bring the children forward in their conceptualizations. But what is going to provoke a learner to modify present ideas is unknown until the interaction unfolds. Therefore Ms. Connolly, in order to provide the most appropriate education at any time for any student, must invent her plans on the spot and adjust follow-up lessons accordingly. This on-the-spot teaching is in no way whimsical or capricious. It is purposeful decision-making that springs from a deeply understood pedagogy.

Many teachers want to control children's performance and want to provide premade devices, such as paper worksheets or fill-in tablets. These types of materials often tell us far less about what children know and can do than interactions with them tell us. Giving young children paper assessments, marking them, and giving them back is largely a procedural activity, with the teacher learning little about the children's conceptual thinking. Paper worksheets and tests provide children with minimal opportunities to explain what they know. Brief face-to-face interactions with young children in the context of materials and actions or observations of young children in interaction with peers typically yield more information and insight.

THE PURSUIT OF MAKING SENSE

Making sense of our world often takes us down mistaken paths. Children and adults can use inaccurate or partial information to build sensible arguments that lead to mistaken conclusions. But constructivist teachers do not stop there. Constructivist teachers honor the child's logic, provide the missing information or direct the child to find it, and then encourage a sense-making process that includes the necessary data.

Constructivist principles state that learning requires active construction of concepts. Concepts cannot be delivered to the child. Many educators try delivering them and often equate their delivery with learning. But time and again, we discover that a teacher's "delivery" of a concept does not equate with a child's learning the concept. Many educators concerned with children's learning of factual science content question how a child could possibly construct for herself the complex concepts that took great minds many years to generate. How, they ask, would children be able to construct the scientific ideas within Ms. Connolly's lesson on forces?

The answer to that question requires us to specifically define the concepts the teacher was teaching. The children in Ms. Connolly's class do not use the words "air pressure" or "air movement," or even indicate an awareness of a relationship between air movement and air pressure. That is not necessary for the lesson to be effective for preschool and primary school children. Ms. Connolly has no expectation that children would use such vocabulary and she has no plans to introduce those terms.

What Ms. Connolly expects is that students interact with objects (such as bubbles and fans and hair dryers) and observe phenomena (such as the bubbles' longevity, stability, movement, rate of movement, and so forth) and construct relationships (such as waving hands cause bubbles to move closer to the hands). Ms. Connolly, who understands the power of internally constructed knowledge, mediates those interactions by questioning the embedded unifying concepts, highlighting selected language, and honoring children's initiative and design ideas.

DELIVER OPPORTUNITIES, NOT CONCEPTS

Although concepts cannot be delivered, opportunities can. Let's look more deeply into the interactions occurring in Ms. Connolly's class to see, even more closely this time, how children construct the beginnings of very sophisticated concepts with simple materials provided by this analytical, constructivist teacher.

Ms. Connolly creates a setting for learning by formulating questions using the language she hears from the children. She spirals back to children's statements made casually, but only highlights statements with the highest learning potential. And she continually redirects the children's focus on one important conceptual relationship: hand waving and the movement of bubbles. She is creating a space in which children can build an intellectual platform on which to analyze ideas. She does so in order to provoke thought and discourse about forces.

For a conventionally accepted reason relating to what is happening in the bubble investigation, most scientists turn to the famous equation dealing with forces presented in 1737 by Daniel Bernoulli. He proved that the pressure exerted by a fluid decreases as the velocity of that fluid increases, a two-and-a-half-century-old idea that still holds true today. Why is it still true? Because that's the way our world works, both in the physical environment (i.e., air, water, and rocks) and in the living environment (i.e., plants and animals). Bernoulli found out something about the natural forces on Earth, worked at making sense of what was happening around him, and designed a way for other people to think about it with him—an equation. Bernoulli's sense-making process about fluids included wondering about bodily fluids. Are speed and pressure related there? With his colleague Leonhard Euler, Bernoulli poked holes in pipes with smaller pipes to practice, and then poked holes in people's arteries with pointed glass tubes to measure their blood pressure, a procedure that was used for 170 years until a safer, less painful procedure replaced it.

As stated in Chapter 1 so much of what adults present to young people as science is really little more than exercises in following directions. Most experiments are not really experiments but rather tightly controlled exercises in which students reach the same conclusions at about the same time. This book encourages teachers to do something different—to set up opportunities in which children can use safe, nontoxic materials to make new discoveries in their own ways within the framework of the curriculum. This type of teaching is based on the premise that learning requires internally constructed knowledge, not merely an accumulation of information. The human mind constructs knowledge from pieces of information, building notions, concepts, laws, and theories. Information is necessary for the construction of knowledge, but it is not knowledge itself.

HOW WE LEARN DETERMINES WHAT WE LEARN

Is air a fluid? Yes, it is. Does hand-waving provide an example of Bernoulli's principle? Yes, it does. Do bubbles provide an example of Bernoulli's principle? Yes, they do. Children everywhere play with bubbles. Do many of them reconstruct this principle from their play time? No, and the children in Ms. Connolly's class have not yet either. But the children in Ms. Connolly's class are building a platform on which someday they might reconstruct and understand this principle. And today that platform is the stage on which they build their young childhood concept that "forces do things even if we cannot see the forces."

The children in Ms. Connolly's class are engaging in the same type of inquisitive experimentation as Daniel Bernoulli engaged in as a little boy. They are learning science by doing science, engaging in the nature of science, and building practical knowledge that can lead to more sophisticated knowledge later in their lives.

CAN CLASSROOMS REALLY WORK THAT WAY?

Although many teachers value the philosophy and pedagogy described in this book, they also wonder about the practicality of interdisciplinary, problem-based curriculum units at a time when educational policies and practices narrowly measure achievement in science. We are in difficult times. Many teachers question the relationship between constructivist teaching and the preparation of children for success on standardized assessments of basic skills.

Although constructivist classrooms are less frequently found within today's test preparation focus, there exists a research base to support constructivist teaching and allay the worry that such will result in poor test performance (Abbott & Fouts, 2003). Additionally, it is important to document that constructivist learning environments foster learning and academic dispositions that are not formally measured on tests but that contribute to the academic transfer of learning.

In this chapter, we set down some guiding principles of early childhood constructivist science teaching that can take place in numerous settings. In Chapter 3, we peek into the world of novice teachers as they struggle and succeed with a way of teaching very new to most of them, a way of teaching for which many of them have seen few prior examples—the constructivist classroom.

Chapter 3

Learning to Care and Caring to Learn

Science is a domain in which teachers and children can learn to care, both about one another and about our shared world and all of the life within it. In order for science lessons to serve a role in this type of global learning, teachers, as master learners, engage in a cycle of teaching lessons, assessing student learning, and reflecting on their professional practice. This Teach–Assess–Reflect cycle is an ongoing practice in which serious educators engage through the career span.

Young children are naturally young scientists, and the readers of this book are learning to facilitate those young scientists' growth as scientific thinkers as they also facilitate their growth as family members, friends, and young citizens. How we teach is intertwined with and intricately tied to our conceptions of ourselves. For many, a classroom of youngsters and the community of a school may be the first mirror in which we have had to look at ourselves for so long and so hard.

New teachers often struggle with their role in the classroom in terms of authority, respect, and control, often before they can pay direct attention to learning. Their most prevalent questions, quite before their interest in providing curriculum well matched to the child's thinking and skills, are ones that they label as classroom management. Ms. Taylor, Ms. Amanda, and Ms. Lindsay, all novice teachers, question their ability to create and orchestrate an orderly classroom environment:

Ms. Taylor fears: "I am least prepared for the management aspect. I think it will be difficult to manage the children's behaviors."

Ms. Amanda looks for guidance: "I would like to know more about disciplining children and how strict teachers can be, without it being excessive or inappropriate."

Ms. Lindsay yearns for good models: "I have yet to see a really efficient way to manage the classroom. I have often seen strategies that were more harsh than necessary, and I am curious as to whether there is a better balance on how to manage the class."

Inherent in these quotes are the implication that children's behavior needs to be controlled by teacher behavior selected from a set of classroom-management strategies. Also implied in these quotes are concerns of not having productive strategies at hand and subsequently losing control of children's behavior. Indeed, there is reason for concern. Teachers must, for critical safety measures, stop behaviors that are dangerous, risky, or hurtful. This is the adult responsibility, and Chapter 14 discusses ways to organize the science learning environment aligned with physical safety standards.

After safety is assured, teachers need to prepare learners to engage and accept ownership of their own learning, and Chapters 12 and 13 provide curriculum units that maximize the learning potential of the environment and reduce the possibility of inappropriate behaviors.

TEACH–ASSESS–REFLECT CYCLE

This chapter contains journal entries from teachers putting constructivist pedagogy into action as they design and implement science lessons. These entries discuss the teachers' struggles and the hurdles they overcome. The chapter speaks directly and indirectly, at varying levels, to the issues of children's emotional and intellectual safety and to how teachers can attain the competencies embedded in the NAEYC professional standard entitled "Observing, Documenting, and Assessing to Support Young Children and Families."

> *Observing, Documenting, and Assessing to Support Young Children and Families*
>
> Candidates know about and understand the goals, benefits, and uses of assessment. They know about and use systematic observations, documentation, and other effective assessment strategies in a responsible way, in partnership with families and other professionals, to positively influence children's development and learning.

GOOD CURRICULUM, GOOD BEHAVIOR

The long-term goal for all types of lessons, whether of science or other subjects, in any classroom is for children to develop the capacity to control their own behavior, modifying it for the cultural, social, and intellectual demands of the setting. The most important elements in fostering good behavior are the nature of the problem-solving challenges, relevant curriculum, and flexible instructional strategies that the teacher offers. That is, good curriculum is the best way to foster good behavior. When children engage in activities that they deem important, their thinking is generally focused and their behavior is generally on task.

WHEN GOOD CURRICULUM IS NOT ENOUGH

When children's behavior veers into the inappropriate domain for the setting or time, the teacher's immediate judgment is imperative.

Does the entire group require more information, guidance, direction, or other resources? If so, the teacher might call the group together, changing the physical space, the interpersonal dynamics, noise level, and nature of the discourse in the setting.

Are specific children acting in predictably inappropriate ways? If the answer is yes, an entirely different teacher response is likely needed. Perhaps the teacher has already established a cueing system for a particular child. When the child becomes upset or agitated, the teacher may quietly hand him a piece of string to handle or clay to mold, thereby redirecting his inappropriate energy to tactile attention on the string or clay. This silent interaction occurs without disturbing the activity of those children who are focused on their own problem solving. It also minimizes the attention the disruptive child is commanding.

Are specific children behaving out of character? In this case, the teacher may ask them to join her in a discussion, and once they are together, she engages them in figuring out the nature of the problem and in searching for a solution. The manner in which the teacher negotiates the explicit content of the curriculum—for example, plant life in a science unit—and the way in which she negotiates classroom misbehavior—such as one child hitting another child—must be consistent. When both are democratic, based on listening to the voices of all, fostering discourse to understand each other, and collaboratively coming up with acceptable ideas, all guided by teacher leadership, children have the opportunity to learn a process they can eventually adapt by themselves.

ASSESSMENT WITHIN TEACHING

What are examples of democratic assessment based on listening, discourse, understanding, and collaboration? Helping children to find patterns in their everyday reality is a powerful feature of any curriculum, whether science or another subject. Facts and figures and dates and events and phenomena all add up to chaos unless the learner starts a process that searches for connections among the pieces of their world and begins to figure out what is important and what is not in solving any particular problem. To see patterns, one must be on a constant search. Patterns are all around us, but only if we seek to find them and try to understand them. To help the child be on the lookout for patterns in everyday life, teachers must be on the lookout, too.

What else, except the search for patterns, describes assessment within teaching? We need to put the act of making mistakes in its rightful place of importance!

ERRORS LEAD TO TRUTHS

An important assessment strategy of the teacher is to recognize the crucial role of error in young children's learning. Adults may unconsciously regard error as something negative. Five hundred years ago, however, the term "errant" meant a person who was on a journey—a journey to search for truth. But journeys into the unknown often lead people down unfamiliar and potentially unproductive pathways, and missteps are inevitable.

When you are with a child who is in your care, what do you do when you make mistakes? Do you show exasperation with yourself, embarrassment, anger, or shame? Or do you express surprise, like, "I sure didn't expect *that* to happen!" Or "I guessed wrong that time." Do you assess whether any damage has been done and, if so, repair it, and then try again? Now, consider your reactions when the child makes a mistake.

When a teacher supports a child's critical examination of his initial ideas, the likelihood of error is present. If a child is not making mistakes, the child is likely not learning. If young Natasha is simply doing what she already knows how to do, she is likely thinking about it in the same way as she has thought about it in the past and, therefore, not challenging herself to go beyond the comfortable. A teacher must not only acknowledge and welcome mistakes as necessary in the learning process, but the teacher must overtly create opportunities for Natasha to make them, recognize them, and correct them.

We want to let young emerging scientists know, at the very least, that it's okay to make mistakes. Ideally we want to communicate that it is actually more than okay to make mistakes, that it is an expected and necessary part of learning and growth. Through a viewpoint that legitimizes and values the making of mistakes, a teacher would not display on a bulletin board identical worksheets depicting 100% of the questions answered correctly. Those identical, perfect worksheets on a bulletin board show that there were many missed learning opportunities in that science lesson!

THE PRODUCTIVITY OF WRONG ANSWERS

In the normative quest for "right" answers to their questions, many teachers miss the opportunity to have their students articulate the processes they use to get at the ideas they are exploring. In a real sense, efforts to get children to give "right" answers often miss teachable moments that spur children to greater inquiry and deeper understandings.

Original research, with its potential for error, prompts children to work at finding out what they really want to say and finding out how to say it well. Thus, content knowledge and skill development reinforce one another in interdisciplinary investigations and in the sharing of outcomes.

A classroom culture that acknowledges experiments that surprise us and ideas that turn out to be false addresses important issues of scientific ethics: accuracy, looking for evidence, and truthful reporting. The acknowledgment of inconsistencies and discrepancies in one's own thinking often leads to action to resolve them. Wanting to resolve mistakes leads to caring, and caring leads to knowing.

If learning is temporary, developmental, nonobjective, internally constructed, and socially and culturally mediated (Fosnot, 2005) then a learner must spend a lot of time working on problems and generating wrong answers. This is true for the growing learner and the growing teacher.

STRUCTURED REFLECTION

Let us listen in on Ms. Allen, a principal, and Ms. Lopez, a 3rd-grade teacher in her 1st year, after an observation of a lesson. Among many other notes, Ms. Allen had counted the girls and boys who raised their hands in the discussion and the girls and boys whom Ms. Lopez had recognized to share their thinking. Ms. Lopez had not once called upon a girl, although there were girls who had raised their hands. When Ms. Allen shared her data, Ms. Lopez responded, "I never saw a girl's hand up." The conversation continued as the teacher contended that no girls had raised their hands. "I would never do that," she declared. The principal showed Ms. Lopez the classroom diagram and the hatch marks she used to keep track of children's responses. "Here is what I saw."

Ms. Lopez had recently completed a paper on gender bias in classroom practice for a graduate class. She didn't want to think of herself as having engaged in behavior that she does not support. The major question for Ms. Lopez, as is true for most teachers during the novice years of teaching, is "How am I doing?" This was true years ago when one of the landmark pieces of research in the area of career stages was conducted (Fuller, 1969), and is still true today. Although the question in the mind of most new teachers may be "How am I doing?" it is not always easy to accept direct feedback on the question.

Ms. Lopez didn't want to think that she had missed the potential input or marginalized the contributions of the girls in her class. But she had. Her first response was to deny it. It took some time for her to see her principal as a colleague working with her collaboratively to make the children's schooling more productive.

Perhaps more important than accepting feedback from others is the ability to self-reflect. This chapter focuses on the types of structured reflections in which teachers can engage in order to improve practice. Becoming a competent teacher requires structured reflection, a way to process thoughts and feelings about what one is doing in the classroom through the vision of excellence shared by those within the learning community. A teacher must focus her reflections on the features of classroom interaction that are critical to achieving the goals of the classroom. The framework in Figure 3.1 can guide that reflection.

With every new interaction with a child, the teacher needs to revisit her answers to the following questions. First, "What does it mean *to learn*?" and second, "What does it mean *to teach* based on what I know about learning?"

Sometimes a teacher shifts her answers to these questions in a big way. What types of experiences help a teacher question her current thinking? Many of us have heard the following statement from Eastern philosophy: "When the student is ready, the teacher will emerge." In this case, when the teacher is ready, the reflective teacher will emerge.

FIGURE 3.1. Guidelines for teacher reflection.

Knowledge of Subject Matter	I understand general science principles. I see the "big ideas." I adapt the subject and the vocabulary to the learner.
Lesson Planning	I connect lessons to the learning standards. I present problem-based learning situations. I create the "need to know." I establish frequent checkpoints for understanding.
Communication	I question, listen, and respond. I ask children to elaborate on ideas ("Tell us more"). I demonstrate sensitivity to equity issues. I use conventional grammar and syntax. I articulate clearly and with varied tonality. I speak in developmentally appropriate levels of language.
Instructional Strategies	I respond explicitly to students' prior knowledge. I respond to student questions and ideas. I adjust to unexpected situations. I adapt lesson procedures based on observation. I observe safety guidelines. I have professional rationales for my teaching behaviors. I see the "big picture" of the classroom. I am aware of student behavior beyond the immediate area.

The following section provides sample reflections of new teachers who are redefining their concepts of teaching, specifically constructivist teaching, and are reformulating their work in their own classrooms. As you read these excerpts from their journals, think about who is the focus of each reflection—the learner, the teacher, the school administration, or others.

BECOMING A MASTER LEARNER

This section illustrates some of the common responses as new teachers engage in professional development. Responses are grouped according to themes discussed in upcoming chapters and are presented here in order to set the stage for the reader's engagement with those theses as they emerge later in the book.

Unifying Concepts/Big Ideas

"Unifying Science Concepts were a new idea for me [see Chapter 9]. I now have them listed on the science wall in my classroom. I do not expect my students to refer to them, but they are there as my reminder for me. For example, our last unit of study was Plant Life. During my planning for this unit I made sure to look at each of these concepts and incorporate the terms and ideas into the lessons. When talking about plants we looked at the function of different parts of the plants and the order of how these parts help us look into the evolution of plants as systems with order and organizations. I have found that this year's students have built much more knowledge than my classes in the past, and I can see how my own planning and teachings have contributed."

"A change that I will make in my teaching next year is to focus on big ideas in my classroom. I learned how important it is to have a big idea in your mind when building a lesson or unit. It helps you and your students better understand what we will be learning and the meaning behind all activities that we do in the class."

Questions from Many Sources

"I have learned that in a constructivist classroom I need to nurture the nature of the questions and enthusiasm of my students. I feel that by letting the students discover more with the technology provided to us (such as the Internet) we can enhance their abilities to succeed in a developing world. On the other hand I have renewed my love for simple things. It is important to remember that the world around us is science, and finding science in the shopping cart is proof of this. Everything around us has questions waiting to be answered and discovered."

Appreciating the Young Learner

"I realized that in order for me to use constructivist methods [see Chapter 2], I had to turn my class into a student-centered environment. This was very difficult for me. I always felt it was necessary to give all instructions before doing experiments. I now know that children learn best when you let them explore and try to figure out what they are going to learn rather than my telling them and giving them the answers. When doing this in my own classroom, I have learned to guide my children in the right direction without giving them the answers."

Changing Ideas About Control

"When I did a "Fossil Dig" activity with my students I gave them a problem to do and told them that archaeologists have to figure out how to find things and remember where they found them."

Changing Ideas About Confusion

"I have also taken to heart the idea that students cannot learn without first being confused. My students always want Ms. Kim, the other teacher, and I to explain everything right from the beginning. They also constantly say, "I don't get it." When I try to explain to them that I need to see their errors before I can figure out where they need help, they often do not want to do anything. I am trying to help my students to be more comfortable taking risks and being confused. I am trying to talk less about errors and trying to provide learning challenges that allow for different types of right answers."

When to Intervene

"I have learned to step back from their explorations and let them figure things out for themselves. Before this I would tell them step by step what they needed to do. Now I give them the problem and allow them to figure out how to solve it. Sometimes I interject if there is a problem with some groups. Sometimes there are fights or other problems, so I do jump in. It is better than a child crying."

Wait Time

"Never telling my students anything I can ask them to think about"— that is a concept that I had a difficult time implementing. I thought that it was hard to let my class have more control over the classroom discussions. However, I have, myself, grown as a professional through this implementation. I can now give my children the option to take control over their own learning. I am very proud of what my students have been able to discover due to this. For example, I always gave my students the opportunity to think and ask questions, but I did not take enough time to let them answer problems before I told them what they were about."

The Value of Exploring

"I used to think that an experiment in younger grades could only be done as a demo lesson, controlled and completed by the teacher. But I have seen how there should never really be a demonstration because that defeats the purpose of an experiment. The students should have control over their own learning and reach their own conclusions. Even a failed experiment can be a learning experience."

Finding the Science in Real Life

"I have integrated science into other areas of the curriculum, as well as math. I incorporate observations of live animals and plants into math. Students record observations in terms of descriptive writing and poetry. I find my curriculum is much more enriched when I pull science into and throughout it. Lessons have suddenly come alive and I am enjoying the process with my students."

Learning in Small Groups

"Encouraging students to interact with others has also become something that I want to do more. This leads to cooperative learning, giving them the chance to work together to solve a problem. The classroom becomes more of a working place when everyone cooperates and works together. Students also feel more a part of the classroom setting and I want the classroom to be more like this."

Adapting to Children

"I am beginning to appreciate discovery. When my students point something out, I no longer get upset or distracted. I go with it. I welcome students' discoveries and questions. When my students point something out that they notice I get very excited and we begin to discuss that topic and I make a point to explore it. For example, when one of my students pointed out that both of the butterflies' wings are the same, I planned a lesson about symmetry. The students were very excited to learn about symmetry and they remembered the concept because of it."

The Tone of the Classroom

"One of the changes I have made is that I now pay careful attention to how I introduce a topic or activity to the students. Instead of giving the children the information, I present them with a problem and have the children try to solve it. My students at first looked at me like I was crazy and then began to come up with ideas. I have become a facilitator in the classroom."

Active Learning Can Save Time for Deeper Learning

"Test preparation makes it very hard to work constructively. But when working as a substitute for the science teacher last week, we did an experiment relating to lizards and what their skin is like. Being that lizards are cold-blooded, we first had a discussion about cold-blooded animals and we read about them and how they lay out in the morning to "warm up" for the day. We then went outside with thermometers and different materials and as a group tried to figure out which medium would warm up the thermometer faster. The one that would heat it up the fastest will have similar properties to the skin of the lizard. So I handed them the materials and had them figure out how to conduct the experiment. They figured out that they should first take the temperature of the playground and then wrap the thermometers to see which would increase the temperature. Before, I would have done everything for them and had them watch me. Now I know that the students can do much more than I give them credit for."

REFLECTION IN STEPS

Let us review what we have just read in the reflections of the new teachers in the above quotes. Most of the statements are about the teacher's own action and changes within his or her thinking. Many of the changes came about through the teacher's interaction with children and the subsequent adjustment of his or her thinking after seeing outcomes. But the report of the change is through the lens of the teacher. This is the first step.

There is a second step in the development of reflection on practice: The teacher moves on to watching the child with the mental rigor that it implies and requires. Step two reflections require watching young children in action. What does "in action" mean? It means watching the child as he or she:

- solves a self-posed problem,
- tries to help another child accomplish a task,
- initiates conversation with another child,
- responds in a conversation, and
- engages in any of the many activities of daily life.

The next section presents another set of new teacher reflections that move toward step two reflections. The reflections are organized using a thematic structure proposed by a well-known and well-regarded early childhood educator, Lucy Sprague Mitchell.

EVER A LEARNER

Lucy Sprague Mitchell, along with a circle of forward-thinking friends in the early 1900s, decided that schools for young children didn't have to be the dreary places that they were at that time. They needed to be better, and Mitchell set about to change things.

What did Mitchell value? Her mission, as she stated it, was "to keep one ever a learner" (Mitchell, 1916, line 5). The ideals that Lucy Sprague Mitchell espoused many years ago are the ideals that drive cutting-edge institutions and associations today dedicated to the healthy growth and development of young children. Mitchell realized that what emerges as important to share is a vivid illustration of what adults value. The following four human attributes—a zest for living, lively intellectual curiosities, flexibility when confronted with change, and courage to work unafraid—are ones that Mitchell declared as essential to foster in children who attended the schools that she helped to build.

Here are quotes from new teachers as they share classroom examples that illustrate their young students' living the ideals articulated by Mitchell.

A Zest for Living

"My students love doing their independent reading and writing outside in the courtyard. They say that they have more fun reading in contact with nature. They also say that they get lots of great writing ideas when they are outside, no matter if it is windy, sunny, or cloudy. One student wrote a great poem about trees while lying under one, and two more decided to write a letter to the principal about turning that same large tree into a 'peace tree' for the whole school."

"I taught a student to independently pump on a swing. The student's affective domain was animated. My student is autistic. She now requests me to sit next to her on the swings and swing with her, instead of asking me to push her."

"In my first-grade classroom we have a weekly Moment in Science. The students each are able to present one interesting thing that they questioned during their week. In the presentations the students have come up with all sorts of different things, from why a mom changed the type of juice that she buys to how shoes make black scuffs on the floor. The student who questioned his mother's change of juice stated that he did not know why she did this. He directly asked his mother and found that she thought that he did not like the juice anymore because he stopped drinking it so much. The mom decided to change the juice back to his favorite. The boy came in the next morning saying that he was happy that they were learning how to ask questions in school!"

Intellectual Curiosities

"We were doing balls and ramps, the kids were blowing the balls across the floor using straws and measuring how far the ball would go using one breath. Abraham turned and asked me if the ball would have enough power to knock over blocks. I told him that he needed to design an experiment that he could do in the class to figure out his own answer. He took ten blocks and stood them up. He then took his straw and ball and blew. The blocks were knocked down by the ball. I then asked him, 'What would happen if you backed up?' He tried it and found out that the ball was not able to knock down as many blocks the farther he moved away. He said to me, 'As I move back the ball loses strength. Why is that?' This experiment ended up taking two weeks to work on because he posed it to the class and we started to explore it as a class."

"On a recent field trip, the students were busy exploring rocks on the beach. One student started to name each rock using what he had learned in class. Then some of the other students started to group the rocks according to type. They had a wonderful time searching the beach, they found the ones that they could not name the most interesting and tried to compare them to the other ones."

Flexible Thinking

"One day a little boy in my class lost his glasses. I could not find them anywhere. So I asked all of the children in class to help me find the glasses. The children said, 'We are being detectives.' Then they started finding clues. We discussed the clues and how we could go about finding clues and what clues can be used for. We also began discussing having responsibility for our own items. I wound up teaching this lesson instead of teaching the lesson that I had planned. This was a great teachable moment."

Courage to Work

"I would like to think that with all my groups I help to foster risk-taking and help to guide each student to become independent workers.

At the beginning of the year it was difficult getting them to pick out the main idea and other important information from the books I read to them. Recently, the quietest girl in my group, Angel, was the only one in the group to use the strategy of looking back to find the information. She wanted to take the book after circle time and asked me to give her another question to answer."

"My students are four years old, so they are constantly asking questions. We do not have Internet access at my school, so the answer is usually in a book. Where to look is the big issue. One day, Omar was playing with a dinosaur in the sandbox. He asked me what type of dinosaur that was. I know the names of a lot of dinosaurs, but I had no clue what that one was called. Omar decided that we should try to find a picture of that dinosaur in one of our dinosaur books. He picked out a dinosaur book, found a picture of his dinosaur, and then I read the name and some facts about that dinosaur for him. I always welcome questions from my students, I am not afraid to say that I do not know the answer, and I work with them to find the answers in some resource in our classroom."

"One day in class we were talking about animals and how they react when they are frightened. One of the students mentioned that he can relate to the animals because after his grandmother passed away, he didn't want to go to the house anymore because he was scared. But now that he is older, he is more educated about death and loves to go to his grandfather's house because he feels the comfort of his grandmother, whom he misses extremely. Wow! He spoke such powerful words and was so comfortable telling it that the whole class clapped. I was proud that my student felt comfortable sharing and I was proud that the class felt comfortable acknowledging their friend."

This chapter concludes Part 1 of this book, "Science in Early Childhood." Part 2 opens with Chapter 4, "Science as Disciplined Wonder," which details the behaviors and dispositions of teachers who can bring a learning space to life by being models of scientists who wonder about their world.

LANDSCAPES FOR
LEARNING SCIENCE

CHAPTER 4

Science as Disciplined Wonder

Science is a social endeavor. All of life is a social endeavor. A note from a little girl offering her mother some "challenges" and apologizing for "yelling" is depicted in Figure 4.1. What gave her the idea to write a note with challenges?

Perhaps the family eats at restaurants with paper placemats that contain printed brain teasers. Perhaps the child has a teacher who offers the class a new challenge every day. Perhaps the child finds challenges to be something invigorating, or something that takes your mind off problems, or . . . We can speculate a great deal. We likely will not know for sure.

But we do know one thing: The child has constructed some understanding of how she chooses to go about handling some social interaction. All children—really, all people—approach new experiences with a set of beliefs and ideas, many of which we may not even know we have! Somehow we wonder enough about something to construct some understanding—right, wrong, or incomplete—and that understanding is what we work with. This chapter introduces the discipline of wonder. What does that mean? Read on.

FIGURE 4.1. Note from Emily.

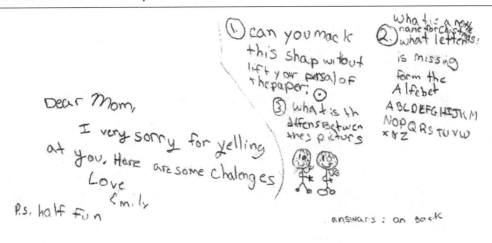

AMAZING IDEAS BEGIN WITH WONDERING

The statement "I wonder" has much power. Teachers can foster their own scientific thinking and that of their young students through "I wonder" statements while using common technology and supplies. A teacher's primary responsibility is to keep alive a child's curiosity about her world. Wondering about the patterns around us is a good place for the teacher to start. Wonder is a discipline rather than a random event (Adler, 1940). The continual search for patterns is one element of the discipline.

The teaching of science, at its most effective, is based on a science of learning. But before a teacher can engage in a thoughtful study of the science of learning (which will be discussed in further detail in the next chapter), an adult must appreciate wonder and curiosity, and reconnect with the wondering child within. We cannot be science teachers unless we can wonder.

Wondering with young children models adult life as inquisitive and growing and as a time of life that might seem interesting to reach! The teacher serves a powerful role in creating an image of an adult culture that values some of the same intellectual playfulness that children very often value. And intellectual playfulness, along with a focus and concentration, is what science is all about.

This chapter looks at NAEYC's (2009) "Teaching and Learning" professional standard from the point of view that the teacher fosters learning through developing a sense of wonder within the learning community.

Teaching and Learning

Candidates integrate their understanding of and relationships with children and families; their understanding of developmentally effective approaches to teaching and learning; and their knowledge of academic disciplines to design, implement, and evaluate experiences that promote positive development and learning for all children.

WONDERING WITHIN THE CURRICULUM

We all need to wonder. And the more we wonder, the more we are likely to find patterns. And the greater number of times we think we see a new pattern, the greater the number of times we can potentially be wrong. But it is also true that the more we wonder, the greater the chance we will learn something new. Let us look at how teachers begin the process of teaching science through "doing" science that addresses the ideas about which children wonder.

Children are often fascinated by and drawn to animals in real life and in photos or stories. Thus, looking at and talking about animals are common occurrences in settings with young children. It is also common to find early childhood science activities using the topic of animals to teach many processing skills. Science kits are typical resources available for teaching science concepts. A science kit usually consists of a box that is prestocked with class sets of materials and a teacher guide for using the materials with children. Resources of this nature often provide specific lessons using particular materials and offering precise instructions. Although these resources can be helpful to new science facilitators, they can also pose a problem. Teachers need much more than science kits and sets of activities in their portfolios, but too often the science kit becomes the portfolio.

Let us analyze two different lessons on animals and look at ways to change the lesson from a compliant use of materials to a purposeful investigation.

CLASSIFYING: WHAT NOT TO DO

The objective of this first sample lesson is to foster children's skills in classifying. Pre-K teacher Ms. Shelley uses a kit designed to teach children how to identify and classify animals using buttons of various sizes, shapes, and colors and a teacher guide showing her how to enhance students' processing skills using the buttons. This activity is commonly used in many settings to begin a lesson on animal classification but is illustrated here as an example of a lesson that often *fails* to accomplish its objectives.

The lesson begins not with animals but with buttons. The buttons serve as a proxy to learn about classification systems before the classification of animals is tackled. Ms. Shelley gives each child a pile of buttons of various colors and shapes and instructs the children to put all the pink ones in one pile, the green ones in another, the purple ones together in a third pile, and so on until all of the buttons are in a pile with like colors.

Scripted plans such as these may initially *look* logical and productive as a strategy for teaching young children how to group according to a particular attribute, a key mental scheme necessary for many types of scientific analyses. Although this lesson seems perfectly logical, it falls short on satisfying the core intellectual needs of children to build a mental model of their own actions. This activity is based on the incorrect assumption that children working with their hands while following directions will increase their conceptual knowledge and then transfer it to another set of objects—in this case, from buttons to animals. This assumption is incorrect, however.

The assumption is incorrect because instructing children on how to manipulate three-dimensional objects is no different than instructing children on how to write and rewrite numbers or letters on paper. While some children may, indeed, enhance their ability to classify from the above activity, it is more likely that most will simply comply with the procedure, establish the right number and type of button piles, and not think too deeply about the meaning of sorting and classifying. Further, we have little evidence that young children engaging in these types of scripted lessons transfer the structure of classifying buttons to the task of thinking about animals.

The precise teacher directions involved in this button-sorting activity most often serve to narrow a child's focus on the task of complying with directions, rather than examining attributes for groupings that make sense. The ability to group any objects or ideas in some meaningful way, what educators call "thinking categorically," is different than following a set of prescribed directions. Both have merit, but they are different cognitive tasks.

How can we change the button activity from a following-directions task to a classifying challenge? How can we encourage the child to think precisely, not narrowly?

CLASSIFYING: ANOTHER TRY

Ms. Shelley could use buttons again. They are available and often attractive to children. But this time she remembers that the original idea of this lesson was to engage children in a classifying problem linked to their interest in animals. It was never really about buttons. Therefore, she moves away from buttons toward something a little closer to the animals—a subject about which the children showed interest.

This time Ms. Shelley provides animal photos instead, and asks the children to separate all of the available animal photos into groups so that each animal is in some group and each group has a name. This challenge offers each child more of an opportunity for conceptual learning than does the previous lesson in which a carefully prescribed set of directions instructs the child on what item to put in which group.

Children bring their best ideas with them when they invent their own strategies for using materials to address problems that they perceive as important. In this second case, Ms. Shelley offers a challenging question through which she can engage the children into ever more precise explanations of their ideas.

CLASSIFYING: INVENTIVE PERSPECTIVES

The classification of animals has a long and interesting history. In 1942, the renowned Argentinean writer Jorge Luis Borges penned an essay on how human beings go about trying to classify everything in our world, even though the classifications we create are arbitrary and full of conjecture. He referenced a classification of animals from an ancient Chinese text in which the following scheme was suggested (quoted in Perneger, 2006, p. 264).

those that belong to the Emperor,
embalmed ones,
those that are trained,
suckling pigs,
mermaids,
fabulous ones,
stray dogs,
those included in the present classification,
those that tremble as if they were mad,

innumerable ones,
those drawn with a very fine camelhair brush,
others,
those that have just broken a flower vase,
those that from a long way off look like flies.

Does this published adult categorization help us better respond to students' inventive perspectives? Teachers' investigations of how and on what basis children form groups can be an important assessment tool that the teacher includes in her science teaching portfolio.

Teaching young children science naturally unfolds in settings with three characteristics:

1. Common materials of children's everyday lives
2. Liberty to ask and investigate real-life problems associated with those common materials
3. Freedom to express one's point of view and change one's mind without fear of being shamed

Ms. Shelley can only create and maintain this setting if she herself can appreciate wonder and is intellectually curious . . . and if she enjoys these same liberties and freedoms.

CLASSROOM STRUCTURE

Let us look at how intellectual settings can be diverse in structure and appearance. One day in Ms. Shelley's room, students might move about the area at free will to gather supplies, work on a computer, confer with the teacher, or take out a project they'd started earlier. On another day, the students in this classroom may be seated, facing in one direction, working on the same puzzle. These 2 days in the same classroom illustrate the variability of classroom structure that is compatible with Ms. Shelley's pedagogy, which values wonder, curiosity, and inquiry.

On a third day, a visitor to this classroom may find Ms. Shelly encouraging three students who just peeked into a bird's nest to share what they saw. In facilitating the children's use of precise language, Ms. Shelley discovers that each child sees something different in the nest. To enhance observational and language skills, she points out the differences among what the children see and suggests, "Let's take another look into the bird's nest together and help each other describe what we see." While observing a bird's nest, Anjali may notice the dog hair, while Ezra may notice the different-colored twigs. All this may be occurring while the other children are working with a guest ornithologist.

These are examples of teaching and learning within environments with spaces for intellectual growth and development, and spaces for academic learning that grows out of intellectual engagement. Ms. Shelley's redefined classroom is an intellectual setting with definite norms, procedures, and policies. But the norms, procedures, and policies are subtle and could easily go unnoticed unless the observer is searching for clues to understand children's intellectual engagement with academic ideas.

Figure 4.2 is a collection of materials that children in Ms. Shelley's class began to put together. In observing the old nests that they had found, Maria noticed that there were tiny bits of yarn or threads in the nests. Maria asked Ms. Shelley if she could make up a basket of supplies for the birds from materials they have in their classroom, then leave it outside for nest building. As you may have already predicted, Ms. Shelley thought that there was lot of learning that could emerge from that idea!

FROM PROCEDURES TO CONCEPTS

Instructing children on *procedures* for academic learning is different than guiding them to more accurate *concepts* for academic learning. What is the difference? Let's look at an example in which a teacher offers guidance but not step-by-step instructions.

Studying plants is another common science activity in early childhood settings, and a common question is "How are flowers different or alike?" As stated in a previous lesson on animal classifications, instructing children on what to look for and how to name and classify what they are seeing can take away the intellectual component of a lesson: The instruction can actually *lessen* the children's chances to build flexible, transferable knowledge. Instead, teachers need to offer children multiple opportunities to build their

FIGURE 4.2. Collecting for a bird's nest.

own classificatory thinking. In order for a child to eventually understand the conventional ideas of how plant parts allow for plant life, a child needs to dabble in being a biologist.

Let us return to Ms. Shelley. How does she conceptually guide a learner? She learns how to proceed from her children. For example, Natasha wonders about the underside of the flower in Figure 4.3. What are the brown petals? Are they petals at all?

Ms. Shelley uses her own classificatory thinking to probe the children's ideas while they are experimenting with different ways of grouping their flowers. She does not rush to share the names of plant parts or information about what functions the parts perform. She does not want to impose a system of thinking that could possibly diminish, rather than enhance, the children's opportunities to look for patterns, build mental models, and construct a larger, more transferable formulation of how to look at other challenges of this nature. Ms. Shelley uses Natasha's observations about what are called sepals to prompt Natasha and other children to think about the life cycle of plants. Ms. Shelley prompts children to look more closely at other flowers that are not fully opened, with petals protected by the sepals. Through helping them see patterns over time, Ms. Shelley guides her students to understand the life cycle of plants and the role that each part of the plant plays.

ARTFUL GUIDANCE

Very often new teachers look at the teaching described above and the structure of the learning environment and ask, How could I manage a group of

Figure 4.3. Natasha's flower.

children if they spend so much time designing their own investigations? How will I know what to say to each child or groups of children? How could I keep everyone focused, on-task, and learning? The answer is called artful guidance. Is teaching an art? Is teaching a science? The answer is "yes" to both questions, and it is at that intersection where artful guidance comes into play.

To guide a learning process, teachers need to know how people build knowledge. In building knowledge, people of all ages engage in similar mental activity. For example, scientists, whether young or old, design experiments, keep track of data, see if the experiment works the same way all the time, talk to other people about their ideas, and find a way to share their conclusions. Let us look at three kindergarten scientists in Mr. Robert's class—Michael, Christine, and Annie—trying to answer their question of which cookie made in the cafeteria is the best.

Comparing Cookies

Mr. Robert is the architect of an environment in which Annie, Christine, and Michael feel invited to pose questions, collect and evaluate information, and test new knowledge. He is also a mentor who establishes frames within which the children test ideas and beliefs. In this case, "frame" refers to the instructional focus of helping children decide a reasonable approach to answering the question "What is the best cookie made in the cafeteria?"

Mr. Robert helps the children frame the question as one that could be answered by investigation. But he is also framing attitudes with which he and the children learn. In this particular case, Mr. Robert helps each child think through the nature and the sequence of their plans by asking about five broad steps in their investigation:

1. How do they want to go about answering their question?
2. What information do they want to gather?
3. How do they know if they are getting good information?
4. With whom do they want to have a conversation about their ideas before they finish?
5. How do they want to share what they found out with the whole class and other important people?

Do those questions sound familiar? They are the same questions that adult scientists ask and investigate. Mr. Robert uses this mental template of questions in guiding his young learners to build their own knowledge about their worlds. Figure 4.4 illustrates how three children responded to Mr. Robert's questions. The children's responses are depicted in vertical columns. Notice the differences in the thinking of each child.

Mr. Robert's goal is to help Michael, Christine, and Annie pursue answers within the premise that science is an evidence-based activity. Through Mr. Robert's guidance, each child forges a unique approach to answering the cookie question. He uses the vehicle of each child's own investigation to offer challenging opportunities to develop children's scientific thinking. This is artful guidance. Each day, Mr. Robert sets a stage for learning and indirectly prompts the activities on that stage.

FIGURE 4.4 Children ask: What is the best cookie made in the cafeteria?

		Student #1 Michael	Student #2 Christine	Student #3 Annie
	Design experiment	Maybe I'll give out a survey.	Should I count what's left over after lunch?	I want to ask all of the girls in the 2nd grade.
	Keep track of the data	I'll just collect the surveys and count up the columns.	Can I ask the cafeteria teachers to let me count all the cookies before lunch and after lunch?	I'll get a notebook and ask all of my friends when they go to the table.
Ask a question → Which is the best cookie from the cafeteria?	See if it works all of the time	Maybe I should do the same thing on two different days and see if I get the same answer.	Do you think I should go to the 1st-grade lunch?	I already know what my friends like.
	Talk to other people about their ideas	Can I work with Jaime?	Can I work with Jaime?	I want to work with Kia.
	Find a way to share their conclusions	I want to make a poster.	I have a camera on my cellphone. Can I take a picture of all the cookies?	Can I give everyone their favorite cookie?

TEACHER AS PROVOCATEUR

Ms. Shelley and Mr. Robert are provocateurs. Some of the children begin their inquiries one way, others in a different way. Ms. Shelley and Mr. Robert are ready for them all. We see them actively listening to Michael, Christine, and Annie and applying a mental discipline of wonder. They have mental templates of how to ask questions, conduct investigations, and document learning that they consistently apply in differentiated ways.

As class time progresses and as the teachers orchestrate the children's sharing of their investigations, the children reveal different perspectives in their study of the same problem. These teachers invite elaboration of ideas and highlight conflicting conclusions for a fuller study by interested children. As students revisit concepts, students transform their knowledge to include more information or increasingly more efficient strategies.

In the cookie problem above, the teacher asks Annie to consider the selection of cookies from children other than those who are her friends. In this case, the teacher is provoking Annie to include more information, information that may differ from her current data. The teacher asks Christine to compare her "before lunch" and "after lunch" cookie counts, provoking her to look for patterns, and possibly generating more efficient strategies for accounting for day-of-the-week or grade-level differences in cookie consumption!

This chapter began with a call for teachers to find the curious learner within themselves and now ends with examples of how curious learners can make good teachers. Learners need teachers who value wonder and inquiry if those learners are to engage in good science. In this chapter we presented images of purposefully constructed learning spaces that nurture children's growth and development and argued for the importance of basing classroom explorations on the overarching "big ideas" of science. The next chapter explores how teachers can foster science learning in various settings, indoors and out, with questions that emerge from the classroom.

Chapter 5

Science Learning Within Family, Community, and Nature

Teachers can enhance the science learning of young children through positive ties with families, communities, and nature. NAEYC (2009) directs teachers to consider the power of reciprocal relationships in its Building Family and Community Relationships standard.

Building Family and Community Relationships

Candidates know about, understand, and value the importance and complex characteristics of children's families and communities. They use this understanding to create respectful, reciprocal relationships that support and empower families, and to involve all families in their children's development and learning.

Scientists go to their laboratories every day for essentially one purpose— to find out something they didn't know before. Artists go to their studios to try something new, mathematicians to their models, writers to their computers, engineers to their test sites, and historians to archives or interviews. Every day, each one has a problem to solve, a challenge to address.

On the surface, a research laboratory of scientists and a primary school of children may seem like two very different communities. In some cases, the distinction may, indeed, be significant. But if the primary school classroom is a constructivist one that engages children in authentic problem solving, the two settings are likely more intellectually similar than they are different.

LABORATORIES EVERYWHERE

Setting up a learning center of any type as a research lab or studio or workshop with interesting challenges offers growth opportunities for the children in that setting. Such learning centers view young children as resident scientists, mathematicians, historians, artists, writers, and engineers, and these environments allow children's naturally emerging competencies to develop and shine. Teaching science means taking a broad look at a child's entire day, not just carving out a "science time" during formal instructional hours. *Where* and *how* and from *whom* we learn is a big part of *what* we learn.

Let's look at a learning environment that is set up to encourage children to work collaboratively to solve an open-ended problem that requires children to intellectually struggle with fundamental physical science concepts and engineering principles. This example uses safe, ordinary materials and can be set up anywhere.

CHILDHOOD PHYSICS: A CARGO-CROSSING CHALLENGE

Young children are often fascinated with trucks, cars, ships, and devices that move themselves or move things from one place to another. Let's analyze how a teacher can set up and implement a challenge that invites children to use selected material and equipment in creative ways to move cargo from one place to another, as illustrated in Figure 5.1.

The teacher keeps in mind the teaching point central to the model of teaching presented in this book: Children are natural problem solvers. Do not foster bad habits by telling them every step to do.

Big Science Ideas

What are the big ideas behind the cargo-crossing challenge? This exercise is about forces and machines. A force is a push or a pull, and a machine is a device that changes the direction of a force or multiplies a force. This notion of multiplying forces is one that requires careful attention by the teacher because the adult must understand it in terms of what it does not mean, in addition to what it does mean, in order not to seed misconceptions in language with the children. A machine that multiplies a force does not mean the machine multiplies the work done or the energy coming out. For instance, a car jack, which is a simple machine we call a lever, allows a

Figure 5.1. Cargo Crossing Challenge

person to press down on one end with a small force, but due to the length of the lever, produce a large force on the other end. We say that a car jack multiplies the force at the expense of distance. The equations of work input and output and force calculations are topics for later in a child's science education. Within this challenge, good science means that teachers explore with children the many ways in which pushes and pulls can be felt, produced, or redirected from the evidence that emerges from activity.

Problem of Emerging Relevance

To begin this challenge, the teacher sets up one area fashioned as a dock and another area to represent a ship. She points to the "cargo" of shells, rocks, and a bundle of fabric, stored in a labeled box, and then offers the following design challenge:

Move the cargo from the (pretend) dock to the (pretend) ship, but you can't touch it with your hands!

Materials:				
rope	dowels	wood	box	spoons
corks	rulers	tongs	spatula	tape
toy trucks	clothespins	paper clips	rake	little fans

Negotiating the Challenge with Children

Young children often put the cargo on a truck and roll the truck, pick up the cargo with a pair of tongs or spatula, use the dowels underneath as rollers, pull the cargo with a string, or tape items together on wheels, among a host of other creative ventures.

The teacher continually reorganizes the materials in order to keep the challenge fresh as new groups of children approach. The teacher may also need to add new challenges for certain children by suggesting partners or putting the ship at a lower position than the dock or further away. With these changes, children must consider the incline of the slope and/or the extended distance and concentrate on more complicated physical science concepts.

Placing potentially incongruent materials side by side can enrich the intellectual environments, particularly if the teacher plans for a variety of responses through questioning and invitations to use supplies in novel ways—for example, "I've seen some people link two cars together." The teacher looks for children's creative use of materials and uses what she learns from one child to challenge other children's thinking. Here's an example: "Kate got the fan to move a box of Ping-Pong balls. But she couldn't get the box of brass tubes to budge. I wonder if it would work if you could combine your method with hers." When possible, the teacher places simple items next to more sophisticated items that are similar, such as a pulley next to some rope and logs, or a battery-operated flashlight next to a magnetic flashlight that a person shakes to charge.

When working with children, the teacher offers needed direction (for instance, on setting up pulleys) or sets up more complex systems (i.e., double or triple pulleys) in order to keep the challenge engaging. As children begin to test various supplies, the teacher observes children's approaches and modifies the challenge with invitations, such as:

> "You two seem to be working on a similar idea. How might you want
>   to work together?"
> "OK. That move was easy. How about if there were no room for the ship
>   dockside and the ship was anchored in the harbor way over there?"
> "What if the cargo was in the basement and had to be moved up a ramp?"
> "Here is a fan. How could this help solve your 'pushing' problem?"

The teacher makes the task more complex, basing the nature of the complexity on an assessment of the child's continued interest, frustration level, disposition to persevere, tolerance of risk, and ability to handle ambiguity.

Additionally, paper bags, little boxes, glue, an assortment of colored pencils, markers, crayons, watercolors, sand, and other natural material collected from seaside can be available as packing supplies. Teachers can invite children to package one of the cargo pieces to "ship out" and take home. The exact challenge and nature of items changes with such factors as the age of the child, time frame, and constraints of the setting. An older child may cut out and fold up cardboard shapes into unique boxes for the cargo, a younger one may paint a picture of the cargo on a paper bag.

Teacher Interactions with Parents

In addition to background in the conceptual ideas of the curriculum, teachers need skills in speaking to parents in respectful ways that help parents to understand the intent and utility of their child-centered classroom. Often parents, eager to help their children, unwittingly solve problems *for* their child through direction rooted in *their* thinking, not their child's perspective. Teachers can describe their work to parents so that parents can understand that it is intentional.

> "I gave your child some dowels, pulleys, and wheels, and asked how he
>   or she might use them."
> "I encouraged your child to try things that I suspected wouldn't work
>   and let her find out for herself. Sometimes she surprised me and
>   used the material in ways that worked!"

Notice that in these examples, the teacher explains how she negotiated the challenge with the child but didn't deliver a solution. The teacher also asks the parent to describe how the child behaves at home with challenges and uncertainties and learns from the parents' perspectives. We call these relationships reciprocal.

Notes from a New Teacher

In the following vignette, Ms. Camp, a kindergarten teacher, reflects on her own engagement as an adult with peers in a teacher-education class in which she "accepted" the cargo challenge.

One day we had the cargo crossing challenge to solve. This wasn't any ordinary problem, but one that could be solved in a variety of ways using an assortment of ordinary materials. Most vividly, I remember having to build a pulley that carried an object about 2 feet to a different location on the table. We had an abundance of different materials from which to choose and use to solve this problem. The materials, other than the pulley shifts, were ordinary objects, including string, toy trucks, rope, scissors, straws, paper clips, et cetera. The problem was challenging. The environment was comfortable and supportive. We knew that the teacher would be there to guide us in the right direction with questions. She would never tell us if we were off topic or not following specifications; she would just question us until we realized what was wrong ourselves.

Appropriate questioning is a technique I find I can learn best through proper modeling. The structure and format of solving these types of tasks become standard. The first minute or so is usually quiet thinking time. I remember thinking, "Can we actually create this? What materials from over there can we use? A straw . . . How can we use the straws to build our pulley system?" On this day, one by one, each group member started to voice his or her suggestions and we would build upon another's ideas to better our design's structure and function. After a couple of minutes, we couldn't wait to get started. I remember the pulley problem most vividly because this was the lesson where I recognized *cooperative learning* in action.

Experiencing It to Know It.

I had read and discussed the concept in many undergraduate and graduate courses, but it wasn't until then that I felt I was a part of what cooperative learning really meant. I recognized the difference between group work and "cooperative learning." My group members and I all felt free to pass along our opinions and try new things. There was no sense of competition or sitting back and letting the others do the work. The problem and project design were so exciting and challenging that we all wanted to be involved. There's the key: making sure the problem given is challenging and interesting. The hard work and preparation of the educator is in designing a problem to hold the students' interests. The preparation seemed intense and I never thought I could facilitate problem-based learning in my classroom with such efficiency and fluency. But then, I had another breakthrough in my own classroom.

Wanting to Share

Each week, I couldn't wait to go to class to find out what we were going to design next. I would anticipate the challenge ahead and looked forward to class. I thought to myself in all honesty, "How many of my students look forward to science class in the same way I look forward to my college science class?" I wanted my students to feel how I felt about science, investigation, and self-discovery. So, I gave it a try in a science lesson on mixtures and properties of mixtures. The lesson was designed so that the students could explore mixtures and determine whether mixtures can be separated back into their original components. (They can.) Well, it was science time and I couldn't wait to see what was going to happen.

Taking a Chance

I gave each group a jar with a plastic cap, sand, and small pebbles. I had the group make a mixture of sand and pebbles and posed the problem. "Using anything in this classroom, how can you separate this mixture?" Since this was new to them, I received a lot of "huh?" and "I don't get it."

It Began to Happen

Then, just as in my teacher education class, one student spoke within the group, and then the others began to feed off of others' ideas and began brainstorming. I saw cooperative learning in action within my own classroom and was amazed. Within a couple of minutes the room was buzzing with science words and learning!

One group punched holes in the plastic cap and began shaking the sand out of the jar like a pepper shaker. The pebbles remained in the jar.

Another group grabbed the screen from the window and began sifting the sand through the screen. The pebbles remained on top of the screen and the sand went into the bowl under the screen.

Another group took the long route and began picking out the pebbles from the sand. Each group member was given a sample of sand to "pick." Although this method was time consuming, it was their way to separate it, and no method of separating was labeled "wrong" or "incorrect."

As I facilitated this event, I was absolutely in amazement. It worked! I didn't think it would fall into place so fluidly, but it did, and the children loved the design work and spoke of science terms and concepts without realizing it. Each group shared its methods with one another. I didn't see anyone acting bored or isolated.

Going Forward

Since that day, I have been incorporating as much problem-based learning as I can in my science curriculum. As the years go by, I am able to include more and build on previous years' problems. I continue to be amazed at how engaged the children are and how problem-based learning in the classroom benefits the students and teachers as learners.

LEARNING IN NATURE

In addition to problem-based learning in the classroom, teachers need to offer children nature-based learning out of the classroom. The importance of outdoor time to children's health and well-being is a current topic of professional conversation and concern. Many cultural factors have led us to our time in history when children spend far less time outdoors than in the past. Fear of strangers, highly scheduled recreational activities, electronic media, and working parents with long hours and multiple jobs decrease the opportunities children have for outdoor time. Some argue that the deficit of outdoor time is a factor in increasing rates of childhood attention deficit disorder, obesity, and depression (Louv, 2008) and that increasing young children's time outdoors can have a positive effect on curtailing these problems (Faber Taylor, Kuo, & Sullivan, 2001).

Moore (1999) and Moore and Wong (1997) suggest that gardening with young children is a healing event that schools and organizations might sponsor. The Children and Nature Network shares research findings that state simply, "Nature is good for children" (Charles, 2009, np). The vision and mission of this organization is to offer a wide range of opportunities for children everywhere to experience nature directly, reconnecting children with nature's joys and lessons, its profound physical and mental bounty.

Louv, chairperson of the Children and Nature Network and author of the well-known book, *Last Child in the Woods: Saving Our Children from Nature-Deficit Disorder*, remarks:

> Will we be the last generation to remember a time when it was considered normal and expected for a child to go out in the woods and wonder? If we take that memory with us when we leave this earth, what will that say about our generation? Or, we could be the generation that chooses to turn the tide. (January 7, 2010, np)

Rachel Carson, the famous biologist and scholar who eloquently wrote about the delicate balances within our ecosystems, highlighted the need for humans to study nature in all of its forms in respectful, unintrusive ways. She is most noted for her careful studies of the effects of pesticides and her courageous call for their careful and limited use, even as she endured strong and continuous attacks by chemical companies. She called for people to live within the beauty and harmony of nature in ways that did not destroy us or other life. She made the case that the key to protecting our world is to see and appreciate its wonder.

> A child's world is fresh and new and beautiful, full of wonder and excitement. It is our misfortune that for most of us that clear-eyed vision, that true instinct for what is beautiful and awe-inspiring, is dimmed and even lost before we reach adulthood. (1998/1962, p. 54)

Within the worldview of Rachel Carson, teachers need to help young children maintain and grow what they already possess—an awe of nature. Thus, teachers can help children learn science and the need to preserve our environment by engaging them in a variety of investigations of nature, indoors or out—but outdoors, at least part of the time.

Nature is everywhere—in rural, suburban, and urban settings. Whether it is a crack in a concrete sidewalk, a planted bed of imported topsoil, or acres of untouched land, plants grow, insects live, and birds fly amid other life activities. And the types of plants, insects, and birds depend upon the locale. Discovering nature around the schoolyard is a way to connect children with nature in ways that foster appreciation and understanding. Nature isn't something that is far away—it is around us at every moment. We have to look to see it. Throughout this book, we investigate ways to foster children's looking *for* nature and looking *at* nature, and building ideas about it.

A simple walk can turn into a hunt to find homes: nests, webs, hives, tree hollows, crevices, piles of brush, piles of rocks, holes in the ground, and puddles of water—all are home to some animal of some type. Children and teachers can take photos of nature and write up their stories and then post them on Wildlife Watch, the National Wildlife Federation's Web site. Classes and families can log on and read together or enjoy the photos.

The National Wildlife Federation has a program wherein teachers can transform schoolyards into certified wildlife habitats (National Wildlife Federation, 2011). Whether you have a small urban playground or acres of free space, you can create a garden that provides food, water, cover, and a place for wildlife to raise their young. Thus, you can help either bring back wildlife or maintain the wildlife in your school vicinity.

MINDFUL ENGAGEMENT

Taking children outdoors can stretch the science curriculum in two ways: beyond the school day and into other areas of learning, such as math, music, literacy, social studies, art, and movement. Children can learn to look up, down, and straight ahead to see different forms of life and life activities. Children can represent what they see in art, music, movement, text, film, or photo. They can compare and contrast bird colorations, features, and calls. They can bring bird and tree and plant guidebooks outside and search to identify what they see. They can watch carefully their favorite species or leaf or twig with binoculars or hand lenses. Children can sprout seeds and plant seedlings in pots or gardens and under different conditions.

In Ms. Camp's class, one group of students wanted to know if watering their plants with water that had been colored red, blue, and purple with vegetable dye would turn the plants red, blue, or purple. The class was eager to arrive at school each morning and see what had happened overnight. Children learn from thinking and talking about what they are doing. This is mindful engagement, and this is what Ms. Camp plans for, fosters, and maintains.

Mindful engagement is the only objective in any lesson plan that is common to all children. The topic, concept, classroom, children, teacher, and parents can all be different in other ways, but the one reason for everyone to be together is to be mindfully engaged in exploring something valued in the community of learners within the classroom and the society surrounding it.

The term "lesson plan" typically conjures up an image of a teacher with a group of students during some time span addressing a certain objective. The class then switches gears to another topic and set of objectives using another lesson plan. This structure may characterize many productive learning settings, but there are also other ways to think about structuring a day in pre-K or kindergarten classrooms. If the teacher has a clear sense of the overall objectives within the larger curriculum, she can spiral through objectives of many lessons, overlapping and creating connections, as she responds to children's statements and inquiries.

Lessons can be chunked into units of study, and units of study can be integrated over different academic areas and over different periods of time. This structure can result in children working on multidisciplinary investigations in shorter or longer periods of time, as a whole class or in smaller groups, or at the same time or at different times. For example, when Ms. Camp integrates nature studies into literacy units, her students develop writing skills as they compare their tiny twigs to the tall trees around them. In her lesson plan book, Ms. Camp codes the one activity as both literacy development and science learning.

A LESSON AS A JOURNEY

Eleanor Duckworth, a student of Jean Piaget and translator of some of his notable publications, is a prominent educator who has contributed much to the field of teaching, especially teaching young children science. Much of her work focuses on better understanding two aspects of both teaching and learning: studying phenomena and collaborating with others who are studying those phenomena (Duckworth, 1996). She conducts her classes for teachers and children in the same way, as research opportunities to study a phenomenon and share emerging understandings with others.

Similar to other educators who honor education as an endeavor rooted in respectful interaction (Malaguzzi, 1993a, 1993b), Duckworth creates learning environments in which the sharing of ideas among learners becomes the basis for extending and refining ideas.

Teaching involves embarking on a journey with the learner, a journey in which teachers invent strategies appropriate to learners and learning situations. Teaching is adapting curriculum—whether published, self-developed, or developed in interaction with learners—to align with how learning takes place. Teachers need not be reluctant to adapt previously prepared teaching materials to the needs of children. Even in schools that pressure teachers to cover prescribed materials and prepare students for tests, teachers can create settings of intellectual freedom within which to learn and teach in meaningful, developmentally sound ways.

This type of teaching requires active listening to students' thinking, ongoing assessments of students, and adjustments to curriculum. These teaching practices, with new examples, are revisited again in each upcoming chapter. They are highlighted in Chapter 8 in a unit on animals and their habitats, in Chapter 10 in a unit on water, and in Chapter 11 in a unit on plants. Chapters 12 and 13 are devoted entirely to curriculum requiring these teaching practices of active listening, ongoing assessment, and negotiation of the curriculum.

The next chapter, "Science of Learning," extends the discussion of early childhood science education in a new context—a deeper look into the "how" of how people learn.

Chapter 6

Science of Learning

The last 2 decades have brought about a new realm of research called the science of learning. Although learning is an array of enormously complex events about which we have much to learn, there exists much research that tells us how to set up places, spaces, and time so as to maximize the likelihood of learning. Countless studies, many hundreds of which were analyzed by the National Research Council, are published in two volumes that are essential for educators: *How People Learn* (Bransford, Brown, & Cocking, 1999) and *How Students Learn* (Donovan & Bransford, 2005). The methods and strategies of science teaching suggested in this book are philosophically aligned with current understandings of how people learn.

CHILDREN'S EMERGING CAPACITIES

Max is near an oven when his mother opens the door. He feels the heat whooshing at him. Later, he tries to take toast out of the toaster and his older sister says, "Don't burn your hand." He likely constructs a silent law, something like, "The closer I get to something hot, the hotter I feel." Later, in his school career, his teacher introduces the notion that the Earth travels around the sun. Max assimilates the new information about the Earth and sun into his old rule that being close to a heat source always makes you hotter, and he comfortably, albeit inaccurately, concludes that it is hotter in the summer because the Earth is closer to the sun.

As Max moves along in school and progresses in his studies of Earth Sciences, he may encounter new information that does not seem to fit with his old rule of "The closer I get to something hot, the hotter I feel." He sees a mismatch and adapts by changing his rule. He may change it to "The closer I get to something hot, the hotter I feel, unless I am much too far away to feel it at all!" So, rather than assimilating the new information into the old rule that has worked in so many other cases, Max does the opposite this time and accommodates his rule to the new information.

NEW QUESTIONS ABOUT OLD IDEAS

Max has ideas about heat. We all have ideas about many phenomena that we have built up over long periods of time; sometimes these ideas are believed to be based on "proof" but actually are based on conjecture. In another example, Max sees that the moon appears to follow him along roads and highways, even as he travels to a different town to see his aunt. Given the perceived "evidence" from looking at the night sky, it is pretty hard to "disprove" that claim. We call this a "naive conception" (Confrey, 1990; Confrey & Kazak, 2006).

Most adults may have moved beyond the naive conception that the moon is following them, but many believe it emits its own light, another naive conception that arises from partial information. People talk of a flashlight brightly shining, and the flashlight is the source of the light. People similarly talk of the moon brightly shining. It looks like the light is coming from the moon! Naive conceptions are powerful because they have been long in the making and they are old ones that we do not readily change. Looking at the moon as a reflection of the sun's light requires the coordination of lots of perspectives and variables, all of which require the moon observer to allow reason to override perception. Learners of all ages need opportunities to question present ideas.

The rest of the chapter illustrates the knowledge base and associated teaching strategies that can help teachers in fulfilling NAEYC's (2009) "Developmentally Effective Approaches" standard.

Using Developmentally Effective Approaches

Candidates know, understand, and use a wide array of effective approaches, strategies, and tools to positively influence children's development and learning.

What do teachers need to know about Max's thinking to positively influence his thinking?

TWO SIDES OF LEARNING

What we witnessed with young Max is what most people would call learning. Jean Piaget would describe it a little differently. Piaget might say that Max is adapting. There are two sides of adaptation: *assimilation* and *accommodation*. When a child's thoughts about his world and his life in his world make sense to him, he is balanced, in harmony, and in a state of cognitive equilibrium. When a child either assimilates new information into existing rules or accommodates existing rules so that he can include new information, he is aiming toward a state of equilibrium.

Piaget's famous work, supported through his detailed observations and measurements of children's thinking, led him to conclude that intellectual growth is a function of a child's ongoing adaptation and modification of present mental structures (Inhelder & Piaget, 1958; Piaget, 1932, 1937, 1947, 1965, 1981). What are these mental structures?

MENTAL STRUCTURES

Piaget theorized that mental structures are sets of coherent frameworks that the human mind builds through maturation and evokes and uses in problem-solving situations. Piaget called these mental structures *schemas*. Others call them mental *skills* or mental *models*. Within the story of the child near the oven at the beginning of this chapter, we called them *rules*. For the remainder of this book, however, we will refer to them as *mental structures*.

According to Piaget's theory, a child's learning is not characterized as the *replacement* of mental structures. Rather, learning occurs through a process of *reworking* and *refashioning* current mental structures, in some cases making them more inclusive, in other cases making them more exclusive, and in yet other cases making them intrinsically different. Piaget called this a process of *reflective abstraction*. A child, through reflection, reconstructs a mental structure into one of greater abstraction.

These mental structures are, of course, invisible to us. The process of reflective abstraction is invisible, as well. It now appears, however, that neurobiological research will someday image these mental structures as sets of connected neural webs that fire in the brain. We know that neurons wired together have conductivity potentials with orders of magnitude above that of a single neuron (Siegel, 1999). When children engage in investigations that require connecting ideas into new systems, they use multiple regions of the brain and develop new electrical connections and neural networks that actually change the physical brain.

Imaging mental functioning in the brain is taking place in research labs around the world. Further discussion of this new domain is beyond the boundaries of this book. But, it appears that today's beginning teachers, as their careers unfold, may encounter fascinating new research about how the human brain works and how what we call "mental structures" today may be imaged as a network of very specific electrical firings tomorrow.

Since at this point in time, however, none of the brain's processing is directly observable, teachers infer what is happening within the brain by analyzing a child's language and behavior.

As children grow, they develop cognitive and social capacities and, thus, at different points in their development, have different cognitive and social needs. What are these unfolding capacities, and what are the needs that adults can fulfill in order to nurture these new behaviors and ways of thinking?

Children have reasons for events in their life, whether they articulate them or not, or whether they *can* articulate them or not. The nature of the reasons they give changes over time. What are the reasons that children give for the phenomena they see—including seeing different parts of the moon on different nights, seeing stars on one night but not the next one, or seeing the sun on a sunny day and not on a cloudy day, watching things drop or fly or spin, seeing people get angry or silly or sad. In the youngest years, a child believes that everything in the world relates to him, and is often controlled by him.

Some researchers call this thinking "magical thinking" (Spock, 2004). Others call it egocentric (Elkind, 1967). Although egocentrism is often associated with early childhood, it pervades development at all ages and stages. It is expressed differently at each stage, but it nonetheless resurfaces. The following brief synthesis of children's developmental patterns with regard to egocentricity is culled from child development specialists whose find-ings have remained similar over the years (Elkind, 1967; Furth & Wachs, 1975; Kamii & DeVries, 1993; National Scientific Council on the Developing Child, 2007; Wadsworth, 1989).

The synopsis highlights the 3- to -6-year period, which is the focus of this book, but also includes the larger birth to 18-year period. Every teacher needs to understand at some level the typical developmental milestones and trends of the growing child to successfully engage with diverse learners with uniquely unfolding skills, dispositions, and aptitudes.

Anna, Birth to Year 2

In the first years of life, Anna learns to physically move and grasp and to emotionally trust. During these years, she learns by handling things, taking pride in her new accomplishments of walking and climbing, and feeling somewhat able to control her environment.

She needs adult interaction for language development, and someone to listen to the new sentences she wants to share and answer her many ques-tions. She imitates what she perceives and needs an adult to construct an enriching environment and provide love and constant interaction.

She needs an adult to set reasonable limits, to respect her, and, equally important, to command respect *from* her.

During these first years of life, as Anna becomes able to distinguish her-self from other people, and distinguish herself from other objects, we say that her egocentrism is decreasing. Anna is a scientist from her first days. Kuhn (1989) sees Anna as an intuitive scientist throughout her lifetime.

Anna, Years 3 to 6

During these years, Anna learns to think in different ways, and her ego-centrism reappears intermittently in terms of her inability to separate her ideas from other people's ideas. Mostly she thinks her ideas are always right! Yet again, just as she learned that other people in the world exist, she now learns to recognize that other viewpoints exist. Even still, she believes that others should be able to understand her even without her finishing her sentences.

Anna's thinking during this period often vacillates between fantasy and reality. She is highly physical and needs freedom to initiate. She can arrange simple series, make simple comparisons, and begin to classify items into groups.

She needs supervision without interference as well as adults to nurture her independence and creativity. Again, during this age range she needs an adult to set reasonable limits, to respect her, and, equally important, to command respect *from* her.

Anna, Years 7 to 11

During these years, Anna learns to play by rules. She wants to make and build things, find out how things work. She can conserve number and length, can classify items into consistent groups and use "when," "if," "since," and "because" in conventional ways. She can apply logical operations to concrete problems.

Egocentrism takes the form of an inability to differentiate between perceptual events and mental constructions. Anna cannot think independently of her perceptions. She is not aware of the distinctions between thoughts and perceptions. Hypotheses requiring perceptually untrue assumptions ("coal is white") cannot be pursued (Wadsworth, 1989). With the attainment of formal operations and the ability to reflect on one's own thought, this form of egocentrism diminishes.

Anna, during these years, needs encouragement from adults who can nurture her self-esteem.

Anna, Years 12 to 18

At this point in development, Anna sees proportions, understands chance, uses "if . . . then" and "either . . . or" in the conventional way, and has the capacity to see other points of view. She thinks about other people's thinking and thinks about what others think.

At this stage, she needs adults who can nurture a concern for the larger society. During this adolescent period, the same egocentric cycle as described in the 7- to 11-year-old period holds true.

We can see from the above accounts that letting go of egocentrism—called de-centering—is an important and fundamental part of both learning and development at all ages. Therefore, to create developmentally sound classrooms, a teacher needs to recognize and understand the process of de-centering, or the capacity to conceive of ideas beyond and not dependent on oneself.

Over time, reasons for events evolve. The reasons Anna may offer for events perceived in her life evolve from ones that are centered on the self as capable of controlling external events, to reasons that are located in a series of events she still controlled, to reasons that are beyond her control and possibly unknowable.

The intellectual, social, and emotional environment in which Anna lives, plays, and learns influences her thinking and behavior. There are so many influences on her development that the term "necessary, but not sufficient" is frequently used in the literature on child development. There are many necessary conditions that must exist for healthy development, but none, alone, is sufficient.

Likewise, we find that there are necessary domains of understanding that a teacher must possess to be a skillful practitioner, but none, alone, is sufficient. The professional knowledge base of a teacher of young children must include a good working understanding of cognitive growth in terms of the stages through which children's thinking develops. However, knowledge of stages is not sufficient. It does not directly inform practice. A teacher must be able to analyze a particular child's reasoning and behavior in order to effectively create settings that might enhance academic achievement, in general, and science achievement, in particular.

REFLECTIVE ABSTRACTION AND THEORY OF MIND

We defined "reflective abstraction" earlier as a child's ongoing modification of her present mental structures, a process that occurs throughout her growth and development. There is another construct, important to a discussion of the development of thinking, which critically informs the work of teachers. It is Theory of Mind (Premack & Woodruff, 1978), a term from a branch of cognitive psychological research.

Theory of Mind refers to the mental capacity of a child to infer what others are thinking, to come to understand that other people have beliefs different from her own and that those beliefs may be true or false. Let's return to Anna. When she can make these inferences, Anna is said to possess a Theory of Mind. As one might expect, this cognitive ability greatly influences her social interactions.

It is thought that the ability to make these inferences emerges in typically developing children at the transitional ages between preschool and primary school ages, typically 4 or 5 years of age (Andrews et al., 2003). Thus, teachers of young children are working with children in transitions that influence how they relate to others and grow intellectually and socially.

Probably the most well-known of the Theory of Mind research rests in the "False Belief Tasks." A researcher sets up a scenario in which a boy puts a bar of chocolate in a drawer and leaves the room. His mother enters, uses a piece of the chocolate for cooking, puts the rest of the chocolate bar in the green cupboard, and leaves the room. The researcher asks the child where the boy will look for the chocolate.

Wimmer and Perner (1983) found that children age 4 and older said that the boy would look in the drawer where he had left it. Children younger than 4 years of age said the boy would look in the cupboard. The younger children could not attribute a "false belief" to the boy. The children knew the chocolate was in the cupboard, and they transferred their correct knowledge to the boy. Children younger than 4 have not yet constructed a Theory of Mind mental structure with which to attribute knowledge different from their own to other people, with false knowledge—in this case, outdated knowledge—being even harder. This major change at about the age of 4 has been replicated in hundreds of studies (Wellman, Cross, & Watson, 2001).

LEARNING THAT TRANSFERS

Anna's understanding of another child's view and her ability to forge social relationships that honor other viewpoints, as seen above, is predicated upon her possessing not only a Theory of Mind, as illustrated in the research studies described above, but also the verbal skills to reach out and be understood herself. Teaching Anna requires the capacity and the power to make ongoing assessments of her understandings and skills, and adjust the curriculum and interventions accordingly.

When Anna spends time in intellectually rich, nurturing environments with skillful teachers, the chances that she will develop the dispositions to want to learn social and academic skills, and the capacities to know when to use them, increase. Equitable learning opportunities often mean resources and curriculum that differ greatly from child to child but that are alike in one important way—they are developmentally matched to the learner. Children in developmentally appropriate settings learn skills that are transferable to the many other settings in their lives.

Too often transfer of learning from one setting to another does not occur. There are many studies documenting some distressing realities. In the 1980s, research reported the problem of "inert" knowledge (Bereiter & Scardamalia, 1989). Students of all ages were not applying school learning in contexts outside of the classroom or within the classroom in different contexts. Their knowledge was inert, neither dynamic nor flexible. More recently, Pugh and Bergin (2005) report very similar findings from studies on the effect of schooling on students' out-of-school experience: School learning has less of an influence on out-of-school experience than expected.

More children are unfortunately spending more time working on activities with little learning potential, with little applicability to any real-world problem-solving situation.

> One might call this the Bo Peep theory of transfer, recalling a couple of the lines from the well-known children's rhyme: "Leave them alone and they'll come home / wagging their tales behind them." As with Bo Peep's lost sheep, the Bo Peep theory of transfer assumes that knowledge and skill a person has learned anywhere will "come home" to wherever it is needed. Just leave it alone. No problem. (Perkins & Salomon, 1990, np)

But research shows us that the Bo Peep theory of transfer isn't valid. Test-preparation curriculums, which are more regularly being introduced into pre-K and kindergarten classrooms, create and privilege one dominant perspective and foster linear thinking. An often stated critique of science curriculum is that it is "a mile wide and an inch deep." Science in the younger grades normatively turns out to be a set of rolling facts in short, clipped, often unrelated sentences. In rare cases, the facts are coupled with "magical" experiments (conducted by the teachers, not the students) that leave students awestruck but with little knowledge pertaining to what actually occurred. We must provide better.

We must attend to the transfer issue directly and with understandings of how people learn. Fromberg reports on the abundant evidence confirming that the construction of meaning is a nonlinear, dynamic process.

> Thus, the significance of content/meaning resides within the learner. A kind of grammar of experience, young children's perceptual/mental images reflect their capacity to distill connections that cross disciplinary boundaries. This transformational grammar of experiences encompasses a holistic integration of socio-emotional, psychomotor, cognitive and aesthetic experience. (Fromberg, 2009, p. 13)

What does this understanding that learning is a nonlinear, dynamic process mean for the early education teacher? Pre-K and kindergarten teachers can facilitate learning by planning spaces in which children can experience phase changes between what they already know and what they perceive as unfamiliar. Encouraging multiple responses to the experience, and multiple representations of the experience, the teacher sets the stage for children to develop stronger, deeper meanings from the experience. Let's explore some ways to deepen the learning value of experiences we provide for children.

Three Rules of Thumb

We can look backward in history to a set of practices that have helped teachers to skillfully negotiate concepts with children for many years. Below are "three rules of thumb" that George Forman and Fleet Hill suggest teachers "tack to the wall" (1980, p. 21), refer to throughout the day, and use as their professional judgment dictates. Years later, the behavioral studies of Kamii and DeVries (1993) also confirm that children benefit when they have sufficient time to observe and make changes first-hand and that their experiences are more important than is the repeating of an adult's verbal description of what is going on. Now, 30 years later, these practices are still valid. Recent insights from George Forman and Ellen Hall (2005) document the enormous learning potential of engaging children in high-level conversations about beliefs, expectations, and assumptions.

RULE #1 "Change Without Exchange." Children learn more about procedures when they physically change something about a single object than they learn from exchanging a single object for another. Forman and Hill offer the example of a child physically making a chair into a rocking chair (which they call within-object transformation) rather than a child sitting in the two different chairs and noting the difference.

RULE #2 "Down with Dichotomies." Children are more able to place opposites on a continuum when given a middle item to consider than they are when asked only to contrast two items, a task that fosters their looking at opposites as discrete extremes. Friedrich Froebel introduced the value of this middle item over 100 years ago when he suggested to add a third item, wooden cylinders, to collections of balls and cubes with which children play and from which they learn.

Forman and Hill agree with the importance of introducing a third item but suggest another feature—the children's own transformations. They suggest asking children to transform a clay ball into a cylinder and then to turn the cylinder into a cube. The children's own transformation of the clay ball into a cylinder and the cylinder into a cube fosters the within-object transformation of the "change without exchange" rule of thumb.

RULE #3 "Classify with Good Causation." Children's logic of action is the foundation of their later logic of spoken language. Children learn more from classifying items within a cause/effect context over which they have control (e.g., classifying objects by how they roll down a ramp when the child releases them). Forman and Hill suggest that this classification activity invites a greater investment in thinking from the child than does, for instance, the attribute blocks and picture cards that children are often asked to classify in preschool (Forman & Hill, 1980). Classification with the blocks and cards is static. But classification of cause and effect that emerges from the children's own research and action is dynamic.

Good Conversations

Based on careful observation of children's current actions and statements, the teacher can begin good classroom conversations with good questions. Teachers listen and watch children to infer what the children believe, expect, and assume.

We might say, "It seems like you think the ball will roll faster if you make the incline steeper." Or we might say, "Do you think you will have more friends if you have crayons?" But then in revisiting an experience with a child, putting that experience into words, we need to go beyond the observed strategies and consider the theories that make those strategies reasonable. "We have to abstract the meaning of elliptical sentences, aborted movements, or a confusing explanation, request, or description. . . ." (Forman & Hall, 2005, paragraphs 10 and 11).

These good conversations are the essence of pre-K and kindergarten classroom science learning: children talking intimately about what they are inventing, discovering, finding out, and constructing.

If we could resist our temptation to put the children on a stage, we might find the real work being done in the wings. If we understood the great value in the ordinary moments, we might be less inclined to have a marvelous finale for a long-term project. We appeal to educators everywhere to find the marvel in the mundane, to find the power of the ordinary moment (Forman, Hall, & Berglund, 2001, p. 53).

NEUROSCIENCE RESEARCH

The behavioral studies referenced thus far in combination with the neuroscientific studies discussed in Chapter 1 frame a convincing argument for the constructivist approaches illustrated throughout the book. The National Scientific Council on the Developing Child reinforces the importance of the learning experiences described within this book:

> Both brain architecture and developing abilities are built "from the bottom up," with simple circuits and skills providing the scaffolding for more advanced circuits and skills over time. Brain circuits that process basic information are wired earlier than those that process more complex information. Higher level circuits build on lower level circuits, and adaptation at higher levels is more difficult if lower level circuits were not wired properly. Parallel to the construction of brain circuits, increasingly complex skills build on the more basic, foundational capabilities that precede them. For example, the ability to understand and then say the names of objects depends upon earlier development of the capacity to differentiate and reproduce the sounds of one's native language. And the circuits that underlie the ability to put words together to speak in phrases form a foundation for the subsequent mastery of reading a written sentence in a book. Stated in

simple terms, circuits build on circuits and skill begets skill. (National Scientific Council on the Developing Child, 2007, p. 7)

The human brain is always changing in relationship to experience. Nobel laureate Eric Kandel (2007) spent decades researching the memory of sea slugs, out of which came significant contributions to our understandings of the biology of what we call the mind, our mental engagement with our world. Our mind and our brain change each other. Human experience in all domains and the dynamics of relationships actually shape human biology (Goleman, 2006). Damasio (1994, 1999, 2003) suggests that emotion and reason are bundled neurologically and that the mind and the body are constantly interacting via biochemicals and neural circuits. Damasio proposes that there exist "convergence zones" in the prefrontal region of the human brain, zones in which electric signals from various parts of the brain converge. He postulates that what happens at this convergence site is complex beyond the capacity of the human genes to handle. He posits that the trillions of electric charges must be directed somehow by the experiences within our environment. Our environment shapes our brain structure by strengthening some of our neuronal connections and pruning others.

Studies by Pinker (1999, 2007) also link the activities of the brain as an organ of the body to the mind as an ongoing process of awareness. The implications suggest that engaging children in science investigations when they are young provides a viable foundation for physical brain development, mindful reason, and positive emotions toward science learning. Sounds like a win-win situation.

While linear correspondences between neuroscientific research and early childhood practice do not exist, there are a number of areas in which early childhood educators can employ strategies that appear consistent with current neuroscientific directions (Marshall, n.d.). For example, we know that prolonged exposure to stress interferes with brain development. Thus, classrooms with predictable routines, clear limits, negotiation of ideas, and active listening can be one example of learning environments aimed at minimizing stress, maximizing learning and, therefore, be in accordance with understandings of brain development. Novelty, contrasting with predictability, "can stimulate the growth of new neurons—a finding that took a long time to win acceptance in the scientific community" (Siegel, 2010, p. 85). Thus, the provision of opportunities for novel encounters may be another example of brain-based education.

CLASSROOM RESEARCH

The importance of science investigations on children's emerging conceptualization of science ideas is well described in *Exemplary Science in Grades PreK–4: Standards-Based Success Stories* (Yager & Enger, 2006). This volume contains multiple stories about pre-K and kindergarten teachers assessing student progress toward the National Science Education Standards through observation checklists that focus the teacher on the nature by which students are demonstrating inquiry behaviors. The following four measures are evaluated by pre-K and kindergarten teachers and are summarized here by the National Association of Elementary School Principals (2009, p. 1).

Does the student:

- Generate questions?
- Make associations?
- Interpret findings?
- Show evidence of understanding?

This checklist can guide teachers in looking for children's patterns of thinking instead of children's acquisition of facts.

The next chapter brings our inquiry into children's learning of science concepts into a discussion of equity issues. How can teachers foster scientific literacy among diverse populations of students in ways that welcome all children into the world of science? Chapter 7, "Liberty and Science for All," documents methods, strategies, and approaches that work in multiple settings.

Chapter 7

Liberty and Science for All

We would like to think that every classroom is a place of liberty and learning opportunity. But, as many disheartening images seen every day on news reports prove, this is not the case. Unfortunately, there is inequity and lack of intellectualism in too many educational settings for young children, particularly educational settings for the poor (Kozol, 2005).

Curriculum geared almost exclusively to test preparation is more prevalent in poor communities than in richer ones (Abbott & Fouts, 2003) and thus serves to further disadvantage children of poverty, who are often children of color. But, every classroom *can* aim toward equity and equality. Teachers using learner-centered, research-based methods, while clearly not solving social ills, can tie state standards with "big ideas" in ways that honor all learners and set the stage to foster meaningful learning. This is as true in poor settings as it is in affluent settings.

This chapter addresses NAEYC's (2009) "Connecting with Children and Families" standard through a discussion of how teachers can reach and teach children with multiple abilities and perspectives.

Connecting with Children and Families

Candidates know, understand, and use positive relationships and supportive interactions as the foundation for their work with young children.

SPACES OF LIBERTY

All schools may not yet be equitable places for all children, but they all can be. The teacher can weave children's diverse comments into discourse that can move the children's thinking and language forward.

Curriculum in the classrooms of these teachers provides spaces of liberty, opportunities for free thought in which children work on solving problems and voice their problem-solving perspectives. Second, the teachers in these classrooms reclaim their role in the class as master learner and steer the direction of the classroom activity and discussion to respond to children's voices.

In order for the positive aspects of diversity of voices to flourish, the teacher must be able to understand how diverse statements about topics and concepts can collapse into unifying principles, keep the learning goals clear, and honor the integrity of all children's thinking. This sounds like a tall order. It is. But, exercising autonomy and stumbling is better than not trying at all. A novice teacher exercising choice and autonomy within the curriculum, even with "rookie" mistakes and shortcomings, creates a more dynamic learning environment than s/he can create when implementing a static rehearsed, paced lesson sequence. A dynamic curriculum, even if imperfect, is better than the lifelessness of a static one. A dynamic curriculum brings openness, intellectual exploration, a forum for diverse perspectives, and the grounds for creative expression. (Brooks, Libresco, & Plonczak, 2007, p. 755)

Teachers must provide opportunities for all children to think deeply about important science concepts as well as the social justice issues that often accompany them. Teachers who introduce these issues into classroom instruction expand the parameters of the curriculum and enrich academic learning.

Neurobiological research has suggested that we can foster complex cognition and enrich learning most effectively in classrooms in which we have established social norms in which children depend on one another as they engage in explorations (Siegel, 1999, 2001). What do classrooms in which children depend upon one another look like? The teacher establishes expectations in accordance with children's abilities to de-center from their own thinking and guides the children to tailor their statements to respond to those from previous speakers:

"So, it sounds like you are agreeing with James and also think the water will get warmer. How might we measure that?"

"Did anyone organize their chart differently than did Julie?"

"We've just heard three reasons to group these numbers together. Let's hear from those who have a different way of computing the total."

As the above examples illustrate, teaching is an intellectually demanding enterprise that requires both intellectual leadership and the ability to orchestrate classroom activity.

THE RICHNESS OF DIFFERENCEs

Classrooms can either cultivate social justice and its composite issues—appreciating diversity, promoting equity, advancing broadmindedness, and encouraging voice and expression—or they can suppress it." (Brooks & Thompson, 2005, p. 50)

When learning settings focus on meaning making, many of the equity problems, which surface in more traditional settings, fall out of the picture. When individual differences based on race or ethnicity, facility with English, abilities or disabilities, or socioeconomic status, among others, are honored as natural elements of a learning setting—not distractions to be minimized or problems to be squelched—each learner has an opportunity for growth at her leading edge.

Diversity of thought and action adds richness to the discourse in a learning setting when the focus is on the making of meaning, which all learners seek to do irrespective of their differences or social capital. Helping young children make meaning is very different than trying to get young children to say the right thing. The focus of meaning making is on getting children to reveal what they perceive as "right" and working with them from there.

CHILDREN WITH LIMITED ENGLISH PROFICIENCY

> The learning of science begins with a child's personal experience of his world, not someone else's interpretation. It begins with questions, not answers; with finding out, not being told; with butterflies and Tinker-toys, not books. (Rutherford, 1991)

Well-taught and poorly taught science lessons differ greatly, as one would expect, and provide very different learning opportunities. Good lessons are always better than poor ones. However, for children with Limited English Proficiency (LEP) in English-speaking classrooms, good science lessons are even better than good. Good science lessons that are constructivist in nature and have an investigatory approach to real-life problems provide a learning platform for language and literacy development, not only science-concept formation.

Let us imagine a group of children hanging bar magnets on strings and observing each other's magnets to answer the question, "Where do the ends of the magnets point?" Using concrete materials, these children interact with one another on a directed task, generating information, sharing it, and needing a way to keep track of the information. Discovering that the magnets all point in the same directions fascinates them, and they draw, sketch, map, diagram, gesture, and talk. All of these activities lead to the natural development of ideas and language. There are many sides of science and they require multidisciplinary skills. When a child has something to say, he finds a way to say it. Research studies call this "scientific sense-making" (Warren et al., 1992) and document the value of this approach for LEP learners.

Science in a constructivist classroom is a way of finding out about our physical environment, which includes all of the nonliving features of our planet and the living environment, which includes all organisms that exhibit the properties of life. Science is inclusive and naturally weaves into language and literacy. Thus, constructivist classrooms in many ways provide full-day English as a Second Language (ESL) instruction. The ESL "teachers" are the children. All of the children, independent of their primary language, are immersed in settings that are designed to enhance everyone's language, literacy, math, music, social studies, art, and science skills. The English-speaking children may be the ESL "teachers" for the LEP children, but all of the children, including the LEP children, are teachers for one another.

Likewise, poorly taught science from textbooks using multisyllabic, specialized words teaches little to English-speaking young children and less to limited-English-speaking children. When hatching eggs, young children do not need to hear or read that chickens are oviparous. But it is part of their education to learn that some animals reproduce by laying eggs that develop outside the body, and when the children see the eggs hatch in their incubator with no chicken present, they will have one example. Children do not need to read or hear that chicks are precocial. But young children can see for themselves that chicks run around a lot shortly after birth. The word "precocial" is not a necessary part of vocabulary development, unless a child is precocious with language and enjoys uncommon words.

What counts, in terms of learning that transfers, is the children's construction of a scenario that can describe an egg's hatching based on the observations the children note themselves. Children who are playful with linguistics may enjoy learning specialized words, and in those cases, the words have meaning. But to copy the word "oviparous," an event seen in many 1st-grade classrooms during a chick unit, has little to do with science and is of minimal importance for the language acquisition of typically developing young children. It is apparent, in any case, that early language develops in specific contexts in which children can point to the situation to which words refer.

CHILDREN WITH SPECIAL NEEDS

All children live on a continuum of strengths and needs, vacillating back and forth at different times and in different domains. Some children live toward the further reaches of the continuum and are often classified as children with special needs. This book offers the perspective that viewing a child as a learner on a continuum is more educationally relevant to and personally respectful of a child than viewing a child categorically.

Traditional schools set up a curriculum with a scope (what is to be taught), a sequence (the order in which teaching will occur), and a pace (the speed at which teaching will occur). Some children have visual, hearing, and motor impairments; intellectual, behavioral, and communication disorders; and/or learning disabilities that make learning within that scope, sequence, and pace overwhelming and, for some, impossible. The accommodations of the curriculum to a child are what we call *special education*, and the accommodations are based on the premise that schools, for certain children, must adapt the curriculum to the child, and not vice versa. This book contends that schools, in their most enlightened versions, adapt curriculum to every child.

Cook, Tessier, and Klein (2007) provide a number of ways to adapt curriculum to the needs of children with special needs. Some examples include attaching photos with names to cubbies and attendance cards for nonreaders, adapting instruments of all types to accommodate students with limited motor skill or low cognition, putting supplies in sequencing boxes for the visually or hearing impaired, and providing simple pictures of feelings or requests for children with limited expressive language. Many of these suggestions are appropriate throughout the age span for typically developing children, as well as atypically developing children.

Classroom structures that can benefit young children with or without developmental delays are said to be in accord with Universal Design for Living (UDL) concepts that provide multiple means of representation, expression, and engagement. UDL is an approach that accommodates learner differences by offering various opportunities for youngsters to participate, learn, and share. Gordon, Gravel, and Schifter (2009) provide an engaging and accessible illustration of the how the GPS system in many cars uses UDL principles to help people get to where they are going. Other emerging technologies allow teachers to customize certain curricular materials to digital, braille, large text, or audio. The National Center on Universal Design for Learning (Center for Applied Special Technology, 2011) supplements selected articles on their Web site with a UDL version that includes hyperlinks with relevant concepts presented in visual and outline form. Rose and Vue (2010) suggest that helping all students learn and succeed requires more than intervening with students. It requires making curriculum and materials more generative and inclusive, and that is just what this book shows teachers how to do. Creating environments of the least restrictive nature produces accommodations that can benefit all children.

From Category to Continuum

Psychologists, social workers, administrators, and teachers within the special education community spend much of their time documenting children's functioning with labels and descriptions of the impairment or disability. Understanding the nature of the impairment is a basis for educators' developing responsive teaching strategies. However, the *category to continuum* perspective situates all learners into a discussion on children's needs, regardless of the degree of the impairment or endowment.

All children interact with their worlds through their senses, whether their senses are highly attuned or limited. All children search for meaning in their worlds based on the information they gather from their senses, whether that information is expansive or narrow. And all children behave based on what they have constructed about their worlds, and what and how and when they are capable of expressing themselves. This is human.

> Children are natural scientists. They do what scientists do, but perhaps for some slightly different and less conscious reasons. They are anxious to understand the world just as adults are. There is a terribly interesting, but rather confusing, world full of stimuli all around them. Many adults, however, have learned to ignore some of that world rather than investigate it. Young children ignore very little. They are very curious; they ask questions constantly. They are willing to look and to inquire about the world. (Worth, 1998, p. 25)

Providing Accommodations

If children look and inquire about their worlds in the ways in which their bodies and brains allow, then teachers of all children need to adjust the curriculum for the learner. Throughout this book, we call this process *negotiating the curriculum*, and depict constructivist classrooms as set up to negotiate curriculum with learners of all abilities. Constructivist science classrooms are supportive of children with special learning needs and children of exceptional learning aptitude because the teacher adjusts her teaching to the unfolding scientist within each child.

In the previous chapter, we discussed Theory of Mind as a developing cognitive capacity that greatly affects social interactions. Hale and Tager-Flusberg (2005), Astington (1993), and Astington and Baird (2005) suggest that autism involves deficits in the child's emerging Theory of Mind, thus accounting for the child's often limited language and communication patterns. With this knowledge, how might a teacher facilitate the science learning of an autistic child?

The teacher might have pictures available along with three-dimensional materials in order to provide a ready avenue for the child to use the pictures in his explanations of what he did or is doing.

Full-spectrum, nonflickering bulbs and materials that absorb sounds can be calming to some children who are highly sensitive to loud noise and flickering light, thus allowing them to focus more readily on a task.

Some young autistic children cannot simultaneously process visual and auditory input. The teacher might show or model an activity without words, then talk with the child using close-up eye contact and no other stimulation.

For children who cannot readily distinguish among hard consonants, an often difficult distinction for autistic children, the teacher can elongate her consonant sounds when she speaks.

These are a few of the many accommodations a teacher can make in the classroom as she comes to understand the exact needs of her pupils.

COLLABORATIVE SETTINGS

How does a teacher provide creative, collaborative settings that can engage diverse populations? It begins with (1) understanding the scientific thinking and developmental needs of the young children in the class and continues with (2) using that knowledge to select appropriate curriculum resources and instructional approaches that can engage children in ways that complement and challenge their developmental levels.

Let's use an example lesson on animals and their habitats to illustrate some basic ways to differentiate materials and instruction:

- The teacher makes available books with pictures and texts of varying abstractions and details.
- Photos of real animals in their homes and feeding areas can provide leading-edge learning opportunities for some children, while maps and legends requiring higher levels of abstract and representational thought can provide leading-edge learning opportunities for others.
- The teacher can make resources available in library areas for children's independent selection or can level and label resources in library areas for guided selection.
- The teacher can also call groups together for instruction with materials that have been preselected for particular children and learning objectives.

Differentiated materials and instruction can help teachers unleash the power of young children's minds within the social parameters of the classroom. Differentiated materials and instruction can help children find order in chaos. Facts, numbers, times, events, and phenomena all add up to chaos unless children start processes that search for connections among the pieces of their different worlds. Facts, such as the names of various parts of animals or flowers, have little meaning outside of a challenge of determining what those parts do. Lessons that merely address facts typically end with a set of new words—with little meaning and no real opportunities to use the words.

Similarly, lessons in which children add numbers with no reference to any objects, such as 4 + 3 = 7, do not typically foster greater abilities to solve the problem of how many boxes of pencils to take out of the closet if each box has two pencils and there are seven children who need pencils. Children begin to figure out what's important and what isn't in solving any particular problem only when they have problems to solve. Creating settings with developmentally appropriate problems is the way classrooms invite engagement of diverse young learners.

THE LEARNING CONTEXT

The *context* within which a child builds concepts influences the depth and the transferability of that child's learning. Context plays a critical role in how young children cognitively and socially develop, learn science concepts, and use their learning. Preschool and primary-school-aged children need the context of everyday "ordinary" occurrences in order to perceive and build patterns about their worlds that inform overall scientific literacy.

Time spent reading and exploring children's picture books is one example of productive time to highlight mathematical, scientific, and technological principles. Through this perspective any classroom activity can become an interdisciplinary investigation. For instance, the watercolors and poetry of *Water Dance* (Locker, 1997) can add a new dimension to a unit on weather, or the study of the properties of water, or an investigation of how matter changes phase. Likewise, a young child's new understandings of water principles can heighten a child's appreciation of the flow of the Locker book.

Studying concepts related to water and linking that study to books such as *Water Dance* may be readily apparent because the topics are the same—both the lesson and the book discuss water. There are also many ways to include good children's literature in the study of scientific concepts, even when the science link to a book is less obvious. For instance, *At the Same Time* (Tirabosco, 2001) can be a delightful book to explore when the children are studying shadows, or clouds or the sky. Children can connect the pictures and text of the book with their studies that measure shadows, track the time of day, describe the clouds, or watch the colors of the sky change.

All of these expansive opportunities to become more sensitive to the phenomena around us are not only opportunities to build science concepts and link them to literature, but are also rich opportunities to develop writing skills (Hapgood & Palinscar, 2007). There are many forms of writing available to young thinkers: diagrams, flowcharts, titles, notes, and so on.

Using writing as a tool to think scientifically and creatively links literacy and science in ways that enhance childhood learning in general.

Providing multiple contexts in which children can engage with the "same" concepts afford greater numbers of learning opportunities to greater numbers of learners, thus creating more socially just settings. Other examples of how teachers can transform everyday events into potentially scientific experiences include inviting children to: look closely at the water droplets on a leaf in a picture (see Figure 7.1), witness the rainbow falling across the room from the window with clinging water droplets, connect the ice cubes floating in a pitcher of water to the iceberg in the picture they viewed last week, and determine whether a paper towel absorbs water more quickly or more slowly than a terry-cloth towel. In the next chapter, we look at how a teacher's ability to differentiate curriculum for different learners is very much related to the teacher's understanding of not only the learner, but the content of the lesson.

FIGURE 7.1. Water on Leaf

Chapter 8

Negotiating the Science Curriculum

A child's active construction of knowledge is an interactive process that is promoted by social contact, with the teacher playing a key role (DeVries & Goudsblom, 2002). What is this role? How do we help children "give up" old ideas that do not work and replace them with ones that do? We negotiate the curriculum!

Learners change beliefs only when they are confused by trying to match new ideas and information with old ideas and information and cannot make them fit. The teacher's role in helping children "change their minds" is another term for the teacher's role in facilitating the process by which children form new concepts. Children come to learning environments not for teachers to "fix" their thinking, but for teachers to create interactive environments in which children refine their own thinking.

This chapter looks at NAEYC's (2009) "Building Meaningful Curriculum" standard by describing some sample lessons and analyzing the degree to which they invite children to engage in categorical, representational, and relational thinking, the fundamental cognitive milestones of early childhood. Teachers who can provide multiple opportunities for children to engage in these mental activities in various science domains provide meaningful curriculum.

Building Meaningful Curriculum

Candidates use their own knowledge and other resources to design, implement, and evaluate meaningful, challenging curriculum that promotes comprehensive developmental and learning outcomes for all young children.

MEANINGFUL CURRICULUM

Meaningful curriculum can only exist in classrooms with teachers who understand the ways in which young children think and understand the degree to which lessons align with the leading edge of how children currently think. Teachers must ask themselves: What types of thinking must a child employ in order to engage successfully in the curricular tasks?

Sometimes, teachers focus on children's interests to the exclusion of other critical factors in meaningful curriculum. Sometimes, teachers want to cover so much science curriculum that they engage in teacher talk that fosters little science learning. In trying to offer meaningful curriculum either tied to children's interests or aligned with curriculum guides, teachers can miss the developmental connection of the curriculum to the children's current thinking and, thus, find themselves teaching science lessons with little science in them.

DESIGNING BETTER SCIENCE LESSONS

Let's look at two different types of science lessons. First, we'll see the types of intellectual engagement Ms. Spencer's preschool "polar bear" lesson invites. Immediately following is an excerpt from a day in which Ms. Spencer taught a lesson she designed as a follow-up to having read a book about animals that live in the cold. We will see that the developmental demands of the curriculum are mismatched to the students. The chapter continues with a look into how Ms. Spencer might reformulate the lesson to include more authentic science and math learning opportunities.

A Developmental Disconnect

Ms. Spencer begins with an introduction that may sound like the start of an experiment but that is not an experiment at all. Notice that she tells the children what they are going to find out before they attempt to find out:

> **Polar Bears actually have black skin, not white. They live in a really cold environment. Black is an excellent heat absorber. However, their fur is clear. They look white because their fur reflects the snow. Today we are going to show that black absorbs heat better than white.**

Ms. Spencer then gives the children thermometers and tells them to put the thermometers under the black paper and the white paper. She turns on the lamps over the papers and instructs the children to wait for 5 minutes. Notice that the experiment is Ms. Spencer's design.

In less than 1 minute, Khalilia and Ben are off to another corner of the room, David and Tom keep lifting the papers to peek at what is happening to the "red stuff" in the tube of the thermometers, and Will and Mary yell at David and Tom for "messing up" their experiments. These behaviors are the behaviors of children who are not intellectually engaged in the curriculum that Ms. Spencer is offering. Ms. Spencer rounds up all the children to listen to her conclusion, not the children's conclusions:

> **Look at this thermometer! The temperature under the black paper is higher than under the white paper. We just proved that black is an excellent absorber of heat. We now understand why polar bears have black skin. Their black skin absorbs heat in their cold environment.**

David and Will put their arms next to each other, comparing skin colors. Fair-skinned Will asks darker-skinned David if he is hot and David asks Will if he is cold. Ben and Khalilia run to the door to greet a teacher assistant who is entering the room. Ms. Spencer calls the children back together and then reveals another trait about polar bears:

> **They have a thick layer of blubber, also known as fat, that keeps them warm. This helps them to stay warm in the cold Arctic climate.**

Ms. Spencer distributes petroleum jelly with the following instructions:

> **Cover one finger with petroleum jelly and then place both your dry finger and your petroleum jelly-covered finger in a cup of ice water. Have your partner see how long you can keep both of your fingers in the water.**

After a few minutes, she tells the children:

> **This experiment shows how important blubber is to keeping a polar bear warm.**

The above lesson is well intended, but misguided. Ms. Spencer (1) plans a lesson with too few ties to the developmental skills of the children in her class; (2) extends the lesson with the blubber activity without indication that the first part of the lesson, the thermometer activity, has fostered her intended concepts; and (3) thinks *for* the children, instead of offering opportunities for them to think for themselves.

The concepts embedded in the polar bear skin and polar bear blubber activities demand a level of de-centering that the children in her class do not bring to the tasks. In the activities of this lesson, Ms. Spencer presumes the children "believe" that the black paper serves as the polar bear's black skin and the petroleum jelly functions as the polar bear's blubber. Hiding things under different colored papers is whimsical and coating fingers with jelly is a kinesthetic carnival. Thus, the children compliantly follow directions. But do they understand the relational logic? Given the lack of planned opportunity within the lesson for children to share their thinking, Ms. Spencer has no opportunity to find out.

Missed Opportunities

In the blubber activity, Ms. Spencer furnishes the reason why a polar bear has blubber: "This experiment shows how important blubber is to polar bear in keeping them warm." She misses giving children opportunities to think about the precursor question: "What keeps polar bears warm in cold weather anyway?" In not engaging the children in articulating their reasons for the observed events, Ms. Spencer misses the opportunity to find out what linkages the children are making. The lesson, as one to learn about polar bears, makes no sense if the children do not see a link between the jelly on their table and the blubber on polar bears.

In the construction paper activity, Ms. Spencer furnishes, not only the reason why polar bears have black skin, but also how black skin works: "Since we now proved that black is a excellent absorber of heat we can understand why polar bears have black skin and how important it is for them to absorb heat in their cold environment." Again, she thinks for the children, not with them, and expects them to believe her interpretation of the evidence.

Science Lessons with Real Science and Real Math

Let's change this lesson to offer children opportunities to ask their own questions, design their own experiments, decide what data to collect that will help answer their questions, and determine how to share what they find.

Science provides an ideal setting to learn, use, and practice the math skills that are imperative to success in science. Let's use the polar bear lesson to foster children's use of technology and tools for problem solving and the development of fundamental skills in measurement. We begin with an opportunity for children to consider the numbers and lines on a thermometer. What does looking at a "higher red column" or a "lower red column" mean? In this new lesson, children need to articulate their reasons for observations.

The temperatures under black paper and white paper exposed to a heat source are decidedly different. Observing a difference can prompt children to ask great questions that can lead to many investigations. But reading a thermometer, an instrument typically calibrated in increments of two degrees, is a skill many children find daunting until well into the upper grades of elementary schools. How can we begin the learning process?

"Reading" a Thermometer

Think about the following: If you have a problem that a thermometer could help you solve, then a thermometer is a good tool. If you want to know if it really does get hotter on a sunny day under a black piece of paper than on top of it, you want a tool that can help you measure "hotness." If you believe that a thermometer can measure "hotness," then it's a good tool for your measuring problem. It can give you the data you want.

There is evidence of logical reasoning and problem-solving in the above paragraph. A child's selection of a thermometer as the right tool for a job, her coming to understand what the changes within the tube mean, and her ability to "read" the changes are fundamental academic and life skills. Thus, rather than asking children to look at the tool while she reads it, Ms. Spencer can give the children the tool, focusing on one big idea: "The red goes up when the 'hot' goes up." With that one line of direction, invite the child to find out if, indeed, it gets hotter on a sunny day under a black piece of paper than on top of it.

Learning to read the various lines on the thermometer can come later. Actually, in every lesson, the children's behavior and comments tell Ms. Spencer when they are ready for more precision.

"Modeling" Polar Bear Blubber

We can also restructure the lesson to engage children in figuring out a way to show that blubber keeps polar bears from getting cold in cold water.

In a discussion with Ms. Spencer, Will tells his classmates, "I saw a scuba diving movie. Maybe the blubber is a little like those suits they put on." Will's statement is a window into his thinking. He is revealing some relationship he perceives between wetsuits and blubber.

Ben and Kahlilia do not see the jelly as a model of blubber. Nonetheless, they are excited about conducting their own investigations of the properties of petroleum jelly and the properties of their own human fingers in cold water. In order to design experiments, Ben or Kahlilia respond to questions that pique their interest. Ben asks, "How long can I keep my jelly-covered finger under cold water?" And it is Ben who decides how he can get an answer to the question he poses. Kahlilia wants to find out how her fingers feel in her snow mittens if she dips her mittened hand into cold water. In these interactions, we see Ben and Kahlilia begin different but related explorations with Ms. Spencer following the children's leads and the children's digging deeper into their own initial investigations of the familiar tasks of putting on mittens or putting on ointments or creams.

With Will and David, who think about the jelly as a model for blubber, and Ben and Kahlilia, who do not, Ms. Spencer structures opportunities for both groups to design their own experiments. She seeks to locate children's learning of concepts within their everyday environment. In effect, learning about insulation begins to occur in this lesson for Ben and Kahlilia without reference to absent polar bears once Ms. Spencer begins to negotiate the original curriculum.

The lesson continues with Ms. Spencer working with the children on various ways to represent their ideas. After they decide what data to collect in each experiment, or what event to watch in their investigations that are observational, the children determine how to document their thinking and Ms. Spencer serves as a facilitator of that process.

THINKING *WITH* CHILDREN, NOT *FOR* CHILDREN

There are a number of different concepts and process skills that can emerge from this reformulated polar bear lesson. Two main science concepts explored in the reformulated lesson are:

1. Temperature tells us something about heat.
2. Properties of materials determine how well they insulate.

Three important processing skills, or ways of thinking, fostered in the reformulated lessons are:

1. Relating objects, events, and ideas to one another.
2. Categorizing objects, events, and ideas.
3. Representing to others what we think.

Using developmentally appropriate language and questions, Ms. Spencer addresses these concepts and skills in varying ways and at varying levels of specificity.

Remember the thermometer lesson? The precision of language changes, but the big idea remains the same: Measurement of temperature is a proxy for heat absorption. The big idea in children's terms may be: "The temperature on a thermometer tells me how hot it is." Remember the petroleum jelly lesson? The children use the petroleum jelly in different ways, but the big idea from the teacher's perspective remains the same: The composition of a material influences its insulating capacity. Children may state the big idea as: "Some stuff keeps things warm or cold. Some stuff doesn't."

Thus far, in this chapter, we have analyzed a teacher's lesson with a group of youngsters in terms of how to address science questions at levels and in ways that invite academic growth, cognitive development, and life skills in general. We see evidence that teachers must not do *for* children what they must do *for* themselves, and must not think *for* children when thinking *with* them can foster greater learning.

When teachers look at science lessons as authentic investigations, and not a set of vocabulary words to be memorized or a set of laws to be repeated, they provide children with powerful opportunities to construct deep understanding: "The method of science, as stodgy and grumpy as it may seem, is far more important than the findings of science" (Sagan, 1995, p. 22).

How might Ms. Spencer, with a reformulated understanding of curriculum, plan a curriculum unit to follow up on the lessons in which she just engaged her class? She must begin with a reformulated and enhanced understanding of the content. She determines that a unit on animals that live in the cold has particular significance in the region in which she and the students live. When the weather turns colder, concepts of insulation become an "ordinary" backdrop for her children's lives. Similarly, concepts of insulation play an important part in the lives of her children when the weather warms and everyone attempts to keep themselves or objects "cool."

The unit she plans looks at penguins, polar bears, and puffins. These animals are similar to one another in that they need to stay warm in order to survive and thus are similar to humans in many ways, as well. But they also have unique features that young children can study and appreciate. Most children find them to be interesting animals, and engage in finding out more about them with interest and enthusiasm.

Thus, in order to think *with* her children and not *for* her children, Ms. Spencer needs to think about the content *before* her children think about it. In order to effectively facilitate a science unit on animals that live in the cold, Ms. Spencer needs background knowledge on concepts of insulation, heat, color, light, and the life cycles and habitats of animals that live in the cold. This section summarizes Ms. Spencer's research.

Once Ms. Spencer started her research on animals that live in the cold and on the physical phenomena that occur between hot and cold areas, she found herself in an ongoing quest to know more. All teachers must engage in these ongoing quests in order to enhance and maintain current and usable background knowledge with which to plan and implement meaningful lessons. Ms. Spencer did not share with her children all of the information she researched, but she built her own knowledge base for curriculum planning and upcoming studies and for questions posed by particularly inquisitive students. Her own active engagement with the ideas of the unit fostered her further active engagement—a learning cycle that is true for any age group.

Insulation

After research, Ms. Spencer looked at the concept of *insulation* from a new perspective. She never knew that human babies are born with brown fat, a type of cell that functions to generate heat. Although our bodies are not as well adapted as are other animals for surviving the cold, we have invented ways to keep ourselves warm. Clothing manufacturers use super-thin, lightweight insulation materials in jackets, gloves, and boots. Buildings are designed with insulation in the walls and double- or triple-paned glass, which traps air. We also use insulation to protect us from other things besides the cold. Think of the covering on electrical cords—a form of insulation designed to keep the current flowing and to reduce the risk of electrocution.

The natural tendency is for heat to move from a warmer object to a cooler one. This is true within our bodies or within a rock, between the ocean and the air, or between coffee and the cup it is in. Insulators cut down on how readily heat can do this. Common insulators that may come to mind are items like Styrofoam or a down quilt. The same insulating material can serve to keep one object warm and another object cold. They do this by reducing heat transfer, which occurs in three main ways:

1. *Conduction*—Some materials, called conductors, allow heat to travel fast, while other materials, called insulators, do not. Metal is a good heat conductor, whereas air is not as good. Many insulating materials are mixed with air to make them better insulators.
2. *Convection*—Convection usually refers to air heating up around a warm object. The heat of an object transfers to the surrounding air. As the air warms, it rises and cool air comes in to replace it. The cool air heats up, causing it to rise, and the cycle continues. This is why we blow across a hot cup of coffee to cool it down faster—you increase the rate at which the cool air comes in contact with the warm object. Insulators usually trap air to prevent it from rising to reduce convection.
3. *Infrared Radiation*—This type of radiation is a form of light that cannot be detected by our eyes. However, just as with visible light (see below), it can be absorbed by certain colors and cause objects to heat up. We can feel infrared radiation on our skin: warmth from a radiator, hot asphalt on a summer day after the sun has gone down, intense heat from a bonfire. About half of the sun's energy is in the form of infrared radiation. Many insulators use reflective surfaces to reduce the contribution of infrared radiation to heat transfer.

Good insulators reduce all three of these forces.

Penguins, Polar Bears, and Puffins

When Ms. Spencer looked into the life cycle and habitats of animals that live in the cold, she decided to focus on three particular ones: penguins, polar bears, and puffins. Why? Without experience, "animals that live in the cold" is a categorical term that doesn't necessarily conjure up a concrete image in a child's mind. However, Ms. Spencer knows that she can bring in books, photos, National Geographic films, YouTube videos, greeting cards, figurines, or toy animals depicting penguins, polar bears, and puffins that can evoke very powerful images. During and after the unit of study, children can determine independently that they all live in the cold.

Penguins have an interesting method for retaining heat. The penguins will all huddle together to protect themselves from the harsh Antarctic winds. As they huddle, those in the innermost part of the group will begin to feel warmth from the other penguins' body heat. As the penguins warm up they will take turns and allow those who were standing in the outermost part of the huddle to go deeper into the huddle and those who were in the inside stand on the outside. They have a layer of blubber that helps them retain heat while swimming in freezing-cold water.

Puffins spend most of their lives flying in the air over the ocean. They fly from August to early spring, at which point they find their breeding islands and settle down for the summer. They survive their winters out over the water through special physical attributes: waterproof feathers that allow the puffins to swim underwater and keep their warmth, the ability to drink saltwater, and finally, by eating small fish and crustaceans.

Polar bears are found in the Arctic, and because they live in such a cold environment, they have ways of staying warm. Polar bears have a thick "coat" of fur. Underneath the fur is a layer of fat. Their fur works in two ways. One, its clear color can be used as a way to blend with the snow and ice. Second, its thick fur is used as an insulator to retain warmth. Polar bears also have fur on their paws to protect them from the cold snow and ice. An interesting fact is that the polar bears' skin is black. The black color can absorb the sun rays to bring heat to the polar bear.

Light, Color, and Heat

The light we see all around us is what we call white light and is actually made up of many wavelengths of light, with each wavelength interacting with our eyes to reflect a different color. Use a prism to investigate for yourself, and consider how and when a rainbow forms. Whenever white light hits an object, three events can happen:

1. *Light waves transform into heat.* Everything on Earth is made up of particles; each particle is made up of smaller packets of energy; and, even if we cannot detect it, everything is always in motion; and thus, everything has what we call vibrational energy. If the vibrational energy of an object exactly matches the vibrational energy of the light hitting the object, the object absorbs the matching light waves and converts the vibrational energy of that light into heat energy.

2. *Light waves reflect backward.* When the vibrational energy of the light waves does not match the vibrational energy of the object,

the energy from the light is re-emitted as light. We see only the wavelength(s) that is (are) reflected, and our brain interprets this as the color of the object.

3. *Light waves pass through an object.* An object appears transparent if the vibrational energy passes through the object until light is emitted to the other side.

Remember that white is all colors combined. Black is the absence of color. White paper reflects all wavelengths of light, so we see white. Black paper absorbs all wavelengths of light so we see "nothing." When we see an object as a certain color, we are seeing the light waves that are being reflected by the object. All other light waves are absorbed.

Thus, Ms. Spencer decides to have both white and black paper available for the children's use in the lesson. White paper reflects all wavelengths of light, and black paper absorbs all wavelengths of light. Thus, black paper absorbs more light energy than white paper.

Camouflage

Camouflage is seen throughout the living environment. While there may be little need to use the terms "predator" and "prey" with young children, it is certainly appropriate to engage the children in noticing how easy or hard it is to distinguish the animals in pictures, for example. In considering the design of their coat, color may emerge as important to the children. This may get them thinking about the color of arctic animals and they may relate their experiments to the importance of the color of arctic animals.

Coloration

Although the color of arctic animals may be related to keeping them warm, perhaps more importantly, coloration is necessary as camouflage. Consider the polar bear, which is well camouflaged in the white snow. Or the arctic hare, which has white fur in the winter and brown in the summer to help it blend into its surroundings. Another interesting coloration scheme is what is known as counter shading. Penguins are a good example of this. In the water, when they are swimming and vulnerable to predators, their white bellies make it difficult to see them from below, while their black backs make it difficult to see them from above.

Survival Strategies

Polar bears actually have two layers of fur. They even have fur on the soles of their feet to protect them from the cold (and to stop them from sliding around on the ice and snow). Some animals avoid the cold by migrating, as is true for many birds, from cold regions during the coldest months and returning when the weather warms up. Some animals sleep through it all— hibernation is a popular way to get from winter to spring. Others, by creating a cozy shelter, can keep themselves warm throughout the coldest times.

Even the overall size and shape of an animal can influence heat loss. Large animals have small appendages, such as ears and tails, which reduces overall surface area and thus reduces heat loss. However, small animals, although they have larger surface areas, do not need as much food for survival, so we often find these smaller animals living side-by-side with bigger ones.

ANIMALS THAT LIVE IN THE COLD: AN EXAMPLE UNIT

With her reformulated understanding of curriculum design and her newly built knowledge base about heat transfer and the life cycles of certain animals, Ms. Spencer plans a unit that builds on her children's prior explorations of insulation, as described previously in this chapter. She opens with a problem-based learning situation.

Problems of Emerging Relevance

The problem-based learning situation here is a design challenge. Ms. Spencer has each child choose a polar animal for the problem, and then she gives each child a small plastic bottle of warm water with the following challenge:

Design a coat for your animal that will keep your animal warm for 5 minutes in a tub of water with ice!

Children are aware that polar animals do not wear jackets, hats, scarves, and gloves, but they enjoy the whimsy of this challenge and apply both dramatic play concepts and scientific reasoning to the production of their "coats."

Materials/Procedures

Ms. Spencer has the following supplies readily available, but waits for children to select them.

Materials:	
zippered plastic bags	petroleum and non-petroleum jelly
feathers	sawdust
polystyrene	shredded paper
batting	cotton balls
ice water	hot water
thermometers	duct tape
clocks, stopwatches, timers	paper

She sets up a 75-watt lightbulb surrounded by a barrier and monitored by an assistant. Safely, under adult supervision, the children can feel the heat.

Also, Ms. Spencer has started a collection of various general materials that are safe, nontoxic, and easy to handle. In this way, she has supplies on hand when children generate ideas she does not predict. She is also open to ideas the children may have. Some children see all the supplies and want to set up a store. Ms. Spencer encourages the "merchants" to sell the production materials to the other children. She introduces simple calculations as the "customers" add up their expenses.

Other children decide they would like to design labels for the coats. With those students, Ms. Spencer introduces diverse types of lettering and logo designs as a way to "read" names. The following site has many age-appropriate resources: www.stemnet.nf.ca/CITE/bearspolar.htm/.

Big Ideas

Open-ended lessons of this type can include the potential for a number of big ideas. In addition to the many ideas about animal life described above, some of the most common general concepts that emerge from this lesson include:

- Animals that live in the cold have different ways of staying warm.
- Different materials offer different levels of insulation.
- Thermometers are tools for measuring temperature.
- Measurement of temperature is a proxy for heat absorption.
- Clocks are tools for measuring time.

Assess Student Learning

The assessment tools that inform teaching are the same tools with which Ms. Spencer instructs. Careful listening to the children's guesses or reasons, asking children to explain their predictions, requesting follow-up to children's original statements, and watching how children select materials and how they use them are all mechanisms by which she assesses learning and determines next teaching steps.

Ms. Spencer uses simple activities and questioning techniques to initiate discussion, much of which includes questions from the children. Honoring all questions, even those not aligned with conventional thinking and those that are seemingly tangential to the specific topic creates an environment that puts inquiry as "standard operating procedure" in the classroom. Analyzing student inquiry is a form of assessment. Ms. Spencer determines next teaching steps by finding out what the children want to know. For instance, when Khalilia suggested that she wanted to put an ice cube in a mitten to keep it warm and Will said that the mitten would keep it cold, Ms. Spencer asked, "Can you show us?"

Children usually begin the design process by testing the insulating properties of various materials. Ms. Spencer asks about how long the children might wait to see what happens. Do they need a clock? How can we read a clock? Would a stopwatch help? What about counting? Can we count high enough?

For some children, talking with a friend is a good recording process. For others, writing is helpful. For still others, charting and graphing this information could be important. Some children develop a rating scale to "grade" the insulating capabilities of different materials. Others decide to ask friends to measure temperature in terms of how cold they think the item is!

Ms. Spencer ends this lesson with ideas she keeps active in her mind for follow-up discussions and investigations as they emerge in the context of other activities.

UNDERSTANDING CONTENT AND COGNITION

As this chapter—and indeed the entire book—illustrates, in order to offer young children meaningful learning opportunities within the context of problem-based investigations, teachers need a solid understanding of the conceptual principles embedded in a topic. Understanding big ideas, not just a set of facts about a topic, is necessary to successfully negotiate the curriculum. Teachers need not be able to answer every child's question, but the teacher, as a master learner, needs the skills to successfully lead a child to resources with answers.

The other important piece of professional knowledge discussed in this chapter, and in this book in general, is the development of deep understandings of young children's thinking and behaviors.

This chapter concludes Part 2, "Landscapes for Learning Science," in which the goals, objectives, methods, and approaches of early childhood science curriculum and teaching practices were described in relationship to each other and in the context of today's current understandings of best practices. Part 3, "From Unifying Science Concepts to Curriculum," is a three-chapter sequence in which the basic foundational concepts of science are described with multiple examples in ways that make these global big ideas accessible to early childhood educators.

Part 3

FROM UNIFYING SCIENCE CONCEPTS TO CURRICULUM

Chapter 9

Unifying Science Concepts

So many things are happening all around children, all around all of us, every day, at every moment. All of us need a way to process these things and make sense of them. How do we do that? We learn to think in ways that help us simplify our lives.

Simplify? you ask. But isn't learning a process of handling more and more information and constructing new knowledge? Yes, it is. But the knowledge we construct is not always only new. Sometimes it is deeper, and deeper means more inclusive, more unifying—knowledge that makes otherwise disparate events tie together into a system that helps us predict events to come.

What are the "simplifying strategies" to make sense of our world—both its living and nonliving parts—that a teacher can use to build her own understandings and facilitate the children building theirs? They are called unifying concepts (National Research Council, 1996), listed below and described in this chapter and the following two chapters.

- Relate form and function.
- Look at whole systems and their order and organization.
- Examine equilibrium and evolution.
- Make models, collect evidence, and offer explanations.
- Measure what changes and what stays constant.

A NEW PERSPECTIVE ON TEACHING SCIENCE

The unifying concepts are not commonly discussed as such, but they are foundational, and once teachers understand them, these concepts can open a new perspective on teaching science and can reconfigure a teacher's conception of what it means to learn science.

If teachers and children engage in the processes mentioned above (relate, look, examine, make, collect, offer, and measure) in the domains mentioned above (form, function, systems, order, organization, equilibrium, evolution, models, explanations, evidence, changes, and constancies), they will generate their own facts from evidence and construct their own knowledge from patterns among facts. That is the essence of this chapter.

All scientists look at elements of form, function, systems, equilibrium, models, and change. Astronomers and Earth scientists study what is very large and microbiologists and nanotechnologists study what is very small. Today, these scientists talk to one another and inform one another's research. Fields of study that were once separated by different research methods, instruments, and background skills are becoming more integrated. Greater numbers of studies link together the once-separate understandings of our world.

Unifying concepts, global by nature and applicable across a wide range of phenomena, emerged from consensus among the many groups who contributed to the National Science Standards. They are the "big ideas" of science, and they serve as the bedrock of science teaching in all disciplines.

Unifying concepts have roots in the everyday experiences of all people, young or old. Figure 9.1 illustrates that there exist a multitude of "common" questions that teachers ask children every day that are questions about unifying concepts. Children can develop strong understandings of concepts and apply them in new settings after they have had opportunities to explore the unifying relationships among the common phenomena around them. The unifying concepts make up the essential ways of looking at multiple domains.

When adults narrate with developmentally appropriate language what children experience, children learn to think within the organizing framework of the unifying concepts. In turn, these experiences rest upon earlier mental process skills such as seriating, relating events, and classifying events that take place as children manipulate and compare materials.

The nature of the questions teachers pose and the vocabulary they use very much influences children's opportunities to extend their own thinking and language. All of us are more able to transfer to new situations the concepts that we built through previous attempts to unify our thinking.

THE SEARCH FOR PATTERNS

As children engage in a study of any topic, we want them to look for patterns. These patterns are the big ideas or unifying concepts. Children become increasingly able to extend their thinking and language when teachers pose careful questions and use helpful vocabulary related to the big ideas. Then, as children see and experience physical events, they become more able to transfer concepts to new situations.

FIGURE 9.1. Unifying concepts and classroom questions.

Unifying Concept	Sample Teacher Question
Understanding the relationship between form and function	How did you decide what tools to use to get such a clean spoon of water from that bucket of dirty water?
Looking at whole systems and their order and organization	You used so many different strainers. Does the order matter?
Examining equilibrium and evolution	How did you get that huge colander to balance on that tiny cup?
Making models, collecting evidence, and offering explanations	How can we prove how much water is left in the paper towel?
Observing what changes, what stays constant, and how to measure them	Your spoonful of water is so clean, but it's so little. What happened to the rest of your cup of water?

NAEYC's (2009) "Understanding Content Knowledge in Early Education" standard stresses the importance of teacher understanding of essential concepts. This chapter describes essential concepts in terms of the unifying concepts that undergird the many topic-specific concepts that an early childhood educator is likely to encounter.

Understanding Content Knowledge in Early Education

Candidates understand the importance of each content area in young children's learning. They know the essential concepts, inquiry tools, and structure of content areas, including academic subjects, and can identify resources to deepen their understanding.

TOPICS, CONCEPTS, AND KEY IDEAS

Let's distinguish among topics, concepts, and key ideas. When we plant a seed and watch a new seedling spring up, we are looking at life reproducing. When we incubate an egg and watch a new chick hatch, we are looking at life reproducing. When we watch a tadpole transform into a frog, we are looking at life reproducing. The notion that life reproduces is a *key idea* from the Science Standards.

Concepts are ideas that state relationships. Young children study the concept that "seeds can germinate without sun" or "seeds can germinate in darkness because they contain just enough food for that process." Young children study the concept that "chicks are born from eggs "or "fertilized eggs need special environments in order for the chick embryo in the egg to hatch and grow." Young children study the concept that "frogs change how they look, how they breathe, and where they live from birth to adulthood."

Seeds, chicks, and frogs are *topics*. They are topics often studied in early childhood settings. Other topics include simple machines, magnets, weather, rocks, fossils, or animals, among many.

In all the examples above, the teacher frames the children's explorations around the more inclusive concept that "living organisms reproduce in different ways" or the even more inclusive key idea that "life reproduces." These two understandings can be brought to an even more inclusive level, the level of *unifying concepts*, multiple examples of which are offered in Chapters 10 and 11. Figure 9.2 summarizes these distinctions.

SIMPLE AND COMPLEX ALL AT ONCE

Science curriculum that puts a few basic, unifying concepts at the center of the curriculum provides three important features: teachers and children can study a few essential concepts in depth, in multiple contexts, and in a manner that facilitates transfer of learning.

The following examples illustrate the types of investigations in which children might engage and the unifying concept that is addressed during that investigation. Notice the unifying concept addressed in each question. These examples illustrate how a teacher can probe children's thinking

FIGURE 9.2. How topics, concepts, and key ideas relate.

Topic	Concept	Key Idea
Frogs	Frogs change how they look. Frogs change how they breathe. Frogs change where they live from birth to adulthood.	Life reproduces.
Seeds	Seeds can germinate in darkness because they contain just enough food for that process. After seeds germinate and become seedlings, they need light to make their own food.	
Chicks	Chicks are born from eggs. Fertilized eggs need special environments in order for the chick embryo in the egg to grow and hatch.	
Rocks	Round rocks may have been rounded after hardening or rounded in tumbling water.	Earth processes involve interactions among air, water, and earth.
Batteries and Bulbs	A bulb will light if it is part of a complete circuit and enough energy is flowing.	Energy exists in many forms.

about common everyday occurrences using examples within the living environment.

- When children investigate what birds eat and what their beaks look like, they are relating form and function.
- When children examine what happens to a plant in a dark room, they are looking at whole systems and their order and organization.
- When children listen to their classmate's thinking about how the crayfish are hiding, they are collecting evidence and offering explanations.
- When children watch an ant balance and carry a crumb of bread bigger than itself, they are examining equilibrium.
- When children notice where various fish in the aquarium spend their time, they are measuring what changes and what stays constant.

Teachers can help children begin to construct working understandings of the unifying concepts when they invite children to engage in the examples above. Below are some examples within the physical environment.

- When children investigate how parts of a wind-up toy work and put one together themselves, or when they examine the form of a bubble maker and the form of the bubbles, they are relating form and function.
- When children notice what happens to ice as it melts on a sidewalk, they are looking at whole systems and their order and organization

- When children listen to a friend's explanation of how she makes ice cream by kneading milk and sugar in a Ziploc bag, they are collecting evidence and offering explanations.
- When children look for a way to balance a plate on a sculpture that the class makes, they are examining equilibrium.

Notice that the unifying concepts addressed in each question are the same as the questions above, yet the topics of the questions are different.

LEARNING FROM SOME GREAT SCIENTISTS

What can we learn about teaching science from scientists? Of course, the knowledge that they create and share changes our world. But beyond that, we need to appreciate the processes by which they gain support for their ideas . . . or don't. What can we learn from Isaac Newton, Alfred Wegener, and Rosalind Franklin?

Isaac Newton: The Apple Story

What can we learn about teaching science from Isaac Newton sitting in his garden in Lincolnshire, England, in 1666, and noticing that the apple from his apple tree fell to the ground? We can learn the importance of providing opportunities for children to fully immerse themselves in the world right around them. Newton came to conclude that the Earth was pulling the apple to it, to its center, and that such an action could also describe how other bodies on the Earth and in the sky interacted with one another. If we want children to begin to create links among what they sense and what they think, we must help them think deeply in the moment.

Fundamental laws emerge from everyday phenomena that are part of young children's lives. Young children experience Newton's famous laws every day, as do we all. These laws are fundamental to our life on the planet Earth. They underpin the essential physical science ideas embedded in the National Science Education Standards. What are they? They are three very big laws, but ones that have applicability to young children.

Newton's First Law. If you hang a picture on a wall and do not disturb it, it will be there the next morning, and the next morning, and the next. A motionless picture will stay motionless unless some force moves it. Objects have a natural tendency to keep on doing what they are already doing. Thus, in the absence of other forces, objects maintain their present state of motion or rest. Newton called this the first law.

It is this first law of motion that explains why we need to wear seat belts. However fast a car is traveling, the passengers are, too. So seat belts help the passengers safely stop along with the car. Indeed, passengers in motion stay in motion in a straight line unless otherwise acted upon. The seat belts lock upon impact, acting upon the person who is beginning to hurl out of the seat.

Newton's Second Law. All of us have likely experienced the fact that it is easier to push a child than an adult on a swing. If you push a child on a swing, the child accelerates in the direction of the push. If you push twice as hard, the child accelerates twice as much. But, if you push an adult who is twice the mass, the adult accelerates half as much. Newton's second law states that the rate of change of the momentum of an object is in the same direction and proportional to the forces acting on the body. It takes more force to move a heavier person than a lighter person through the same distance.

Newton's Third Law. A person stepping off of a boat onto the shore pushes the boat away from the shore with an equal force. Newton's third law states that for every action, there is an equal and opposite reaction. Rockets propel into space in the same way that boats get pushed away from the dock. The engines create a downward force to the ground, and the reaction is an equal force that pushes the rocket up. Thus, whenever one object pushes another, the first object gets pushed back in the opposite direction equally hard.

Alfred Wegener: The Implausible Story

In 1915, Alfred Wegener published an idea that we know today to be accurate, but not complete. Wegener proposed a theory of continental drift, and his colleagues thought his ideas were implausible. Yet Wegener, with his partially true ideas, is credited as a founder of the plate tectonics theory, far earlier than he had the tools to prove it.

For many years, Wegener wondered why the continents of South America and Africa appeared to fit so neatly together. He hypothesized that they must have, at one time, been attached. Knowledge of identical fossilized plants and animals on each continent convinced him that his theory was correct. He could not, however, explain how the continents had moved. In today's thinking, we know that the continents themselves are not moving, but that the crustal plates on which the continents and the oceans lie are moving. Today, we attribute the movement of the plates to convection currents that begin in the Earth's molten interior. And indeed, today's geologists concur that at one time on our planet, all of the continents were together as one big mass. Today, all of the continents are still moving.

Teachers can learn from this story that what we may originally think is implausible may turn out to be a great idea in the making. Therefore, we must resist immediate judgment of new ideas and allow the idea maker some time and resources to further explore.

Rosalind Franklin: The Tenacity Story

In the early 1950s Rosalind Franklin spent endless hours in her basement laboratory X-raying pieces of DNA, trying to determine its structure. Her photographs began to point to a double helical structure of the DNA molecule, but she didn't think her photographs proved it well enough. While she was trying to produce better photographs, Francis Crick and James Watson thought the X-ray photographs she had already prepared in her laboratory were conclusive enough, and they developed a 3-dimensional model of the DNA molecule based on those photographs and their own ingenuity and published their findings. This is a poor story of equality or professional courtesy, but it is a good story of tenacity.

Franklin's tenacity showed the world DNA for the first time. She has never been widely recognized for her contribution because she died of cancer in 1958, and was not included in the 1962 award of the Nobel Prize in Physiology and Medicine that went to Crick, Watson, and another colleague, Maurice Wilkins. But her contribution was profound, and this story reminds teachers that science requires perseverance. Rosalind Franklin's resolve to prove the structure of DNA with physical evidence opened a new world of biological science. Her perseverance denied her recognition, but it gave her the proof that she sought.

COLLECTIVE SCIENTIFIC THINKING

The scientists discussed earlier all made major contributions to our collective scientific thinking. Each of their contributions can be analyzed within the framework of the unifying concepts. Can you see where? If you need some ideas, read Chapters 10 and 11 and come back to the question. Chapter 10 details the unifying concepts within physical environment topics and Chapter 11 describes them within living environment topics.

Chapter 10

Unifying Concepts: The Physical Environment

Amelia plays a game of catch. How does she know where to stand and where to put her hands to catch the ball? If Amelia catches the ball most of the time, she not only has developed the physical coordination and strength to do so, she has also put together a lot of ideas about how objects move through space. Amelia has constructed a system that allows her to predict where to put her body and hold her arms. She may not be able to articulate what she is doing, but her competence is a pretty good indicator that she has woven many concepts into a workable system.

We now look at physical environment topics, again through the lens of the unifying science concepts:

- Relate form and function
- Look at whole systems and their order and organization
- Examine equilibrium and evolution
- Make models, collect evidence, and offer explanations
- Measure what changes and what stays constant

RELATE FORM AND FUNCTION

How many beans can I pick up in 5 seconds, once with a fork and once with a spoon? How come newspapers are made of thin paper with rough edges, and books have fancy covers and paper with even edges? Why are some rocks shiny and others dull?

Ms. Penner can focus young children's attention on the connection between *form* and *function* in all domains, not just science. There are lots of questions and challenges that can provoke this type of thinking.

Form and function are complementary aspects of everything in the natural and human-made world. The form of a fork functions as an eating utensil for certain foods and not for others. Its form influences what type of food can readily be eaten with it. The shape of an object or system is frequently related to its use, operation, or function.

Function typically relies on *form*. Understanding this *form–function* relationship applies at different levels of organization. In the physical environment, garden tools, kitchen gadgets, craft materials, and office supplies open up possibilities to directly investigate the *form–function* connection.

LOOK AT WHOLE SYSTEMS AND THEIR ORDER AND ORGANIZATION

Ms. Penner engages students in tasks such as tracking the increasing volume in a rain gauge, collecting rocks of different textures, or contrasting materials that change shape in water with those that do not. Although the complexity and number of parts of any system can and do differ, the general definition is the same: a system contains parts that behave in an orderly way.

Science progresses on the assumption that the behavior of our universe is predictable and based on the same rules everywhere. Discussions of systems within the physical environment include examples such as *systems* of machine parts making an engine run, celestial bodies revolving around each other, and so on.

Systems have distinctive parts or features: for example, nuts and bolts of machines or planets, stars, and moons of a solar system. *Systems* also have a flow of some type of resource: the path of electricity in a machine, perhaps, or the energy flow of celestial orbits. This flow represents the *order* of one aspect of the system. In a *system* of airline routes, there exist pathways and hubs through which people "flow" for work and pleasure. Connecting among these hubs represents an *order* in the system.

To provide useful ways of thinking about our world, we have created *organizational* structures that we use to talk about science. We have classifications of all objects and phenomena, to name just a few: rocks, geological structures, and weather conditions.

EXAMINE EQUILIBRIUM AND EVOLUTION

Ms. Penner, on the playground with her class one morning, notices three children balancing a teeter-totter, with two on one side and one on the other, as she casually passes by. In the classroom later that morning, she sets up a balance and places some masses of different sizes near it. She may informally comment that it reminds her of the teeter-totter. But without further discourse, children approach the materials and attempt to model their teeter-totter play outside.

Change, balance, and *equilibrium* have tremendous conceptual import in classrooms with young children, and Ms. Penner plans for activities that foster that conceptual development.

Equilibrium is a physical state in which forces and changes occur in opposite but balanced directions. In our world, interacting units of matter of all types tend toward equilibrium.

Evolution is a series of changes, some gradual and others sporadic. Although evolution is most commonly associated with the biological theory that explains the process of change due to random mutations from common ancestors, evolution also describes changes in the universe. Walks along the beach over the changing seasons show an evolving coastline. One summer the walk may be along a beach of 50 feet of pink sand from the high tide mark to the boardwalk. Perhaps after a fierce winter storm the walk along the same beach the next summer reveals 20 feet of pink sand.

The landforms, which we can see, and the ocean floor, which we cannot see, *shift* as an outcome of our Earth's constantly moving system of crustal plates tending toward *equilibrium.*

Extreme events like earthquakes, tsunamis, and volcanoes move us toward *equilibrium*? How? We experience those events, and even milder events like mountains getting higher, when the movements of plates of our Earth's crust release a buildup of pressure, a release that tends toward *balance* of pressure.

The water–rock cycle is an example of *equilibrium.* If water is always dissolving rock, what happens to all the dissolved rock? Why isn't the ocean filled up with rock? Why haven't the continents just dissolved and disappeared? In teaching young children, the teacher needs to focus children's attention on the "big ideas" of a cycle—when rock is dissolving in one place on the planet, new rock is being formed someplace else. The rock cycle is in *equilibrium.*

MAKE MODELS, COLLECT EVIDENCE, AND OFFER EXPLANATIONS

Ms. Penner provides rich learning opportunities by inviting children to engage in the types of thinking from which explanations can emerge, and she provides authentic materials with which children can work to generate explanations. She helps children use "real things" whenever possible to make models. Some teachers, for example, want to model the Earth's different types of soil and sand using crushed chocolate cookies for "dirt" and graham crackers for sand. Why? Aren't real soil and real sand filled with learning opportunities? Yes, they are. Thus, Ms. Penner chooses real soil, not crushed chocolate cookies, and real sand, not graham crackers. She keeps it real.

Evidence consists of data upon which to base scientific explanations. *Models* help scientists and engineers understand how things work. They take many forms. *Models* can be physical objects larger than the object being modeled or smaller than the object being modeled. We can use tin foil to *model* how a boat stays a float.

Models can be diagrams or equations or mental constructs. Earlier, we saw how children make sense of their world through the development of mental models. We use models to help us *explain* what we see happening.

A teacher might read books with the children looking at construction equipment and then ask them to use the toy equipment to show how each one works. Some children may want to make their own model of one of them—a crane, perhaps. One concept may be "Some machines make it easier for us to lift weights." With the children using or making miniature machines, the teacher can prompt them to consider how to measure what they mean by the word "easier." With this question, the teacher plants some intellectual seeds for the children's eventual understanding of mechanical advantage as they get older.

MEASURE WHAT CHANGES AND WHAT STAYS CONSTANT

Ms. Penner provides countless opportunities to narrate and question the nature of the *constancy*, *change*, and *measurement* involved in science and mathematics lessons, but also lessons of almost any nature. When children are sifting rocks and sand, she positions small *measuring* cups near the activity and wonders out loud how many little cups of sand come out of the final filter. Or when children are pouring water, she places a thermometer nearby, or plasticware that is very narrow and very wide in diameter. Often, the children need no prodding. Children will most often use the measuring tools out of sheer desire!

Everything in our world is in the process of becoming different. Everything is *changing*. Yet these changes often occur so that something else may be *constant*. Changes can occur everywhere. Water spreads out on a table tending toward equalizing the pressure; ice cream melts at room temperature tending toward equalizing the heat. Even the changes can change: Ice cream melts at room temperature, but it melts more quickly on a hot day.

Changes in systems can be *measured*, and the measurement often clarifies the evidence of change and the formulation of new scientific explanations. There are different systems of *measurement* for different purposes, and deciding when to use which one is an important decision for the learner. When do you use a ruler, a cup, a balance, or a spring scale? Knowing what tool you need is as critical as knowing what to do with it when you have it.

PLANNING A LESSON USING UNIFYING CONCEPTS

We have looked at the unifying science concepts with multiple examples and now conclude this chapter by describing a physics unit in which children study water.

As Ms. Corrado begins to plan a water studies unit, she researches the big ideas of the unit and writes an informative explanation of the science concepts for herself. Why? She does so for the same reason that Ms. Spencer in Chapter 8 engaged in her own research on animals that live in the cold. A teacher cannot teach what she does not know. Oftentimes new teachers ask a mentor for guidance on curriculum planning: "I need to do a lesson on water." But upon the mentor's probing, it turns out that the new teacher needs to learn more about what makes water so special on our planet before she and her mentor can discuss how to teach associated concepts.

As stated in Chapter 8 about Ms. Spencer's self-study, Ms. Corrado's self-study of the science concepts is a critical moment in the lesson-planning stage. The unit of study largely focuses on content areas that include (1) the phases of the water cycle, (2) the conditions under which matter changes phase, and (3) the principles of heat transfer, among other related concepts.

These concepts include profound principles on which our world works. They can be expressed on adult levels. Yet they are also accessible to young children in many varied and relevant ways with simple materials. Ms. Corrado needs a working knowledge of the basic science content in order to offer learning opportunities with the greatest potential. If she lacks a good enough basic understanding herself, the chance to plant misconceptions arises and so does the chance that a child's creative and insightful ideas very much on the "right track" can be overlooked.

In this example, Ms. Corrado begins her lesson planning by first engaging in her own study of water—not to gather facts but to look for patterns. She visits museums, searches PBS for videos, and browses through educational catalogs for indicators of important ideas. She reads books—first children's books, then a high school text, perhaps, or popular science journals. Her inquiry springs from the intellectual platform of the unifying science concepts. She filters the new information through the broad science concepts that unify information into patterns.

Does Ms. Corrado need to be an expert in every science unit? No. That would be impossible. But she needs to know enough about the big ideas of the unit to be the model of a master learner. That is possible and necessary.

WATER STUDIES: A PHYSICS UNIT

Teacher clarity of the big ideas is necessary for Ms. Corrado to meaningfully adjust the lesson for children's different developmental levels and experiences. She must understand both the precursor concepts and the advanced concepts. Offering a student a differentiated learning opportunity requires fluency of teacher thinking.

What is the "big idea" of today's water studies lesson? One big idea of this lesson addresses phase changes: that ice (solid phase) changes to water (liquid phase) if enough heat is added. Granted, if still more heat is added, the water changes to water vapor. But the original lesson did not plan on going that far unless, of course, the children took it there. Duration of attention is largely related to the degree of meaningful engagement. This is true for children of all ages, even for very young children of preschool age.

To maximize the likelihood of the children's meaningful engagement Ms. Corrado needs a clear lesson focus. She needs to pinpoint the major concepts through which she will connect the learning invitations to the children's experiences. She must also make sure that she focuses children's attention on the processes that are emphasized in the National Science Education Standards. The teacher must guide children to:

1. organize the information they collect,
2. talk with other children about what they are finding out, and
3. collect evidence for what they think is true.

Without a teacher's clear goals, discourse and activities can too easily lose direction and become aimless. How does a teacher fill in the gaps of her own scientific knowledge as she prepares to create lessons for young children? Teachers must continually engage in their own research. Books published by the National Association for the Education of Young Children (NAEYC) such as *Exploring Water with Young Children* (Chalufour & Worth, 2005) are one type of resource. Middle school, high school, and college texts are another genre, and television documentaries and online interactive software are a third type of resource.

Big Ideas

The unifying concepts help Ms. Corrado explore specific concepts related to water, the concepts important to a teacher's background understandings if she is to maximize her ability to create lessons and create discourse most likely to result in children's learning.

Let's look at what Ms. Corrado learned about water in terms of the unifying concepts in order to teach the water unit. She learned about how the form of water influences the function it might be able to perform.

- Water in the *form* of vapor (steam) can serve many functions. For example, it is used in steam engines. The pressure from the steam forces a piston to move. The piston is connected to devices that can function to turn the paddle wheels of a boat, turn the wheels of a train, or move a belt to transport goods in a factory.
- Water in the *form* of liquid can also serve a number of functions. For example, it can turn a waterwheel to grind grain into flour.
- Water in the *form* of ice can serve numerous functions. An enjoyable one for children is a skating rink.

Ms. Corrado learned about water's role in the system we call Earth.

- Water is part of virtually every *system* on Earth. It is part of every cell in all living-body *systems*, part of every agricultural system and economic system that makes any product, part of the recreational system of the skiing industry.
- Water temperature can be measured in degrees. The salinities of bodies of water can be *measured* in concentration levels.
- We call the accumulated water vapor and crystals in the sky clouds. We organize clouds into a classification *system* using Latin names—cumulus, stratus, cirrus, nimbus—and further distinguish clouds by the height of the cloud base.

Ms. Corrado studied some of the mechanisms by which water reaches pressure equilibrium and how many aspects of water characteristics evolve over time.

- "Water seeks its own level" is an old adage that can be used here. The pressure of water is determined by the height or depth of the water. Connected water bodies seek to achieve *equilibrium*, and move in ways to reach the same heights. The aqueducts built in Ancient Rome were based on this principle.
- Water quality *evolves*, water pollution *evolves*, and water uses *evolve*. The evolution of water itself is a constantly studied question, with present-day investigations focusing on changes in the water concentration of the Earth's mantle, the massive region just below the crust that extends down to the Earth's core.

Measuring what changes and what stays constant was another inquiry in which Ms. Corrado engaged in order to prepare herself to teach the water unit.

• Under the natural conditions on our Earth, water is one of the few substances that we encounter in three different forms in temperatures in which most animals live: solid water (ice), liquid water (water), and gaseous water (steam or vapor). Whereas the amount of water on the Earth has been the same (*constant*) for hundreds of millions of years, its form constantly *changes*.
• We can *measure* many aspects of water and its *changing* forms, such as temperatures at which changes of states occur, densities of water in its various states, and so forth.
• In fact, water is the basis for the metric system of measurement. One gram of water (its mass) equals one milliliter of water (its volume), or one cubic centimeter of water. We *measure* heat in calories: one calorie is the amount of heat required to raise the temperature of one kilogram of water by one degree on the Celsius scale at one atmospheric pressure.

Finally, Ms. Corrado found out much about model making, and what constitutes good ways to collect evidence and offer explanations.

• What is the *evidence* that makes us think that what we know is true? In science, we test our ideas and collect enough *evidence* to confirm that our results are predictable. What happens when we add heat to ice with all other conditions being equal? We get the same results every time. We produce the same graph, which is our *evidence* of many principles that *explain* phase changes.
• Sometimes *models* provide the *evidence* we seek for answers to questions about the past. The *constancy* of water on the Earth over time is supported by mathematical *models* accounting for phase changes, atmospheric conditions, and extrapolations from data on the *evolving* Earth's surface, among many other factors.

Problems of Emerging Relevance

Water is an ever-present fascination for young children—for all of us. It is all around us in different forms, is part of our world and our bodies, and is a safe and inexpensive model with which to learn about other matter. How do we begin our exploration of this wonderful substance? Here, Ms. Corrado translates the big ideas into a challenge. She asks the children to design an "ice cube keeper," a container that would keep their ice cube from melting for as long as possible. Her discussion with each group as they work focuses on how they plan on keeping the heat from getting to the ice cube. She asks the children to keep track of what they are seeing happen in the ice cube keeper and to the ice cube.

Materials/Procedures

This part of the planning process requires the gathering of materials necessary for the students to carry out their investigations of the problem, accounting for all safety considerations.

For the water studies lesson, Ms. Corrado provides ice cubes, plastic cups, tinfoil, polystyrene pieces, newspapers, tape, et cetera. She has thermometers and stopwatches in the supply cabinet but does not bring them out. Why not? The children's determination of what tools they need to solve their problem is an important part of the process of solving the problem.

In little time, students encounter a host of splinter problems that emerge from trying to solve the original one. One group becomes concerned with what they could use to keep track of time. After talking with each other and their teacher, Ms. Corrado wonders out loud if they could use anything in the room. One of the children looks around the room and determines in an excited tone that "We could use the class clock to keep track of time!" Another group decides that they could use a thermometer to measure temperature. Knowing there would be a question of size, Ms. Corrado directs them to the wall thermometer. When the thermometer is too big to fit into the cups, two sets of sparkling eyes open wider and two children in unison exclaim, "We have little ones!"

These moments of insight are behavioral indicators of the mindful engagement so necessary for success.

It is easier for a teacher to recognize timely openings in which she can connect the children's thinking to other content domains if some materials are collected before the unit begins. For this water studies unit, Ms. Corrado finds an interactive Web site with a problem similar to the ice cube keeper problem, but in the virtual experiment the task is to keep a jar of hot water hot, instead of keeping an ice cube cold. (See http://www.bbc.co.uk/schools/scienceclips/ages/8_9/keeping_warm.shtml/.)

She also finds a number of other virtual experiments that link water to its use in plant growth and other related topics. (See http://www.bbc.co.uk/schools/scienceclips/ages/5_6/growing_plants.shtml/.)

There are many works of literature that can provoke children's pattern seeking and connection making, as well as evoke images and references to other times, places, and phenomena. For example:

Water Dance (Locker, 1997) highlights the aesthetics of the changing states of water within our natural environment.
Come On, Rain! (Hesse, 1999) engages the reader in the joy of a rainstorm during the hot summer.

Assess Student Learning

The children went about their designing and experimenting with quite animated and directed behaviors for the rest of the afternoon. The next day, their work continued with some children bringing in material from home.

The lesson stretched over 3 days, taking over most of the morning each day, and led in varied directions. Ms. Corrado's responses to the children's many ideas naturally connected science, math, technology, and language arts.

Assessment in Service to the Learner. The way in which Ms. Corrado responded to each child was a function of her assessment of how far she could stretch them. Her assessment was in service to the children's learning. She helped some learn to read the big hand of the clock, others to count by twos on the thermometers, still others to glue two sides of the ice cube keeper, and some children to spell the words they wanted to use to describe what they were observing. Learning to read a clock, skip-counting, gluing techniques, and spelling were not on Ms. Corrado's "water studies" lesson plan per se. But, those skills are part of the children's long-term learning goals and emerged as appropriate for specific children as determined through teacher analysis of children's questions, frustrations, or comments.

Extracting Principles from Classroom Events. The children in Ms. Corrado's class ran into many sets of great problems, all of which provided learning opportunities for measurement, spelling, vocabulary, addition, subtraction, writing, and a host of other skills and concepts. Teachers need to be able to extract the basic organizing principles from the many concrete questions, activities, and events in the classroom.

Experiences and feedback provide opportunities for children to bridge transitions and begin to develop the cognitive underpinnings that allow for further growth and development. It is important to note that cognitive schemes cannot be taught. But teachers can provide the types of experiences out of which a child constructs the cognitive schemes when the child is biologically ready. The next chapter looks at the unifying concepts as they relate to living environment topics.

CHAPTER 11

Unifying Concepts: The Living Environment

Exploring nature with children, an important dimension of a teacher's role in early childhood science education, was introduced in Chapter 5. Today's children spend most of their day and night indoors. The inspiration of the well-known naturalist Rachel Carson (1962, 1965) and the strategies of the approach by child advocate Richard Louv (2008, 2010) provide a focus for how we can help children develop an appreciation of nature.

Relationships with others and with nature change how we think (Goleman, 2006). First, developing an appreciation of nature is foundational. Rather than teach about global warming, for instance, plant a vegetable garden and infuse gardening time with a discussion of the benefits of growing food in the community. Creating an emotional connection with the nature of one's own community is key to protecting the global environment and learning more about it.

Second, we should explore nature all the time, not only on sunny, warm days. There is much to learn in damp, foggy, rainy, or windy weather. Birds, insects, leaves, and flowers look different in different environs. Soil, pebbles, sand, concrete, bricks, and macadam do, too.

Third, look straight, up, and down as you explore nature. You will observe different activities on different levels. You will notice the very big and the very small, and the very still and the very active. Use all of your senses and bring along tools to help you—magnifying glasses, audio and video taping devices, pads of paper and crayons, collecting boxes, flashlights, and so forth.

There are many wonderful books available that can help the new teacher develop her own appreciation for natural cycles and phenomena and become more facile with ways to engage the young learner (National Arbor Day Foundation, 2007; Worth & Grollman, 2003).

As we did in Chapter 10 in reference to some key ideas within a study of the physical environment, we now look at the living environment, again through the lens of the unifying science concepts:

- Relate form and function.
- Look at whole systems and their order and organization.
- Examine equilibrium and evolution.
- Make models, collect evidence, and offer explanations.
- Measure what changes and what stays constant.

RELATE FORM AND FUNCTION

The skeleton of a present-day chick is very similar in *form* to some fossils found in the Earth and thought to be very old. This prompts some people to wonder if the body of the fossil performed the same *functions* as that of the chick.

Teachers can focus the young child's attention on the *form-function* connection in all domains, not just science. There are lots of questions and challenges that can provoke this type of thinking, such as "Let's see if we can find out what these animals eat by looking at their mouths." Or where they live. Or what the climate is like.

LOOK AT WHOLE SYSTEMS AND THEIR ORDER AND ORGANIZATION

Our universe is filled with *systems*: we have *systems* of species living together and depending on one another as predators and prey, organs in a human body working together, plants pollinating each other, and so on. These *systems* have distinctive features and a flow of some type of resource: In a *system* of rosebushes, dogs, rabbits, and worms living together, there exists a food web through which energy flows.

To provide useful ways of thinking about our world, we have created *organizational structures* that we use to talk about science. One typical way to organize any set is to create categories.

- We have ways to categorize organisms by what they eat: some species eat animals and some do not, and we have a special name for those two categories.
- We can categorize plants that thrive in the dry desert and plants that thrive in the humid tropics, and we have special names for those categories.
- We have creatures that live in the ocean, most of which are fish but some of which are mammals. There are myriad ways of classifying objects and ideas.

We also *organize* by levels. For example, communities are made up of populations, populations are made up of organisms, organisms are made up of organs, organs are made up of tissues, tissues are made up of cells, and each level engages in the same metabolic processes. This is a very big idea in science!

Although the complexity and number of parts of any system can and do differ, the general definition is the same: a system contains parts that behave in some orderly way. We, as a society, have organized our thinking about these parts. We have mutually agreed upon some conventional language as a way to facilitate our discussion about the parts and our understanding of them and how the parts interact.

Therefore, teachers of young children have important opportunities to question the nature of the *systemic*, *orderly*, and *organizational* structures of our world when young children engage in investigations such as tracking the growth of a bean plant or comparing plants with different types of leaf edges or shapes or arrangement of leaves.

EXAMINE EQUILIBRIUM AND EVOLUTION

As stated in Chapter 10, *Evolution* is a series of changes, some gradual and some sporadic. Although evolution is most commonly associated with the biological theory that explains the process of change due to random mutations from common ancestors, evolution also describes changes in the universe. A group of children taking a shortcut over the front lawn for 1 month on the way to the swings gives rise to a footpath—the grass evolves into a footpath and the footpath evolves from the stepping on the grass.

Equilibrium is a physical state in which forces and changes occur in opposite but balanced directions. The terms "steady state," "balance," and "homeostasis" can also be used. Homeostasis, from the Greek meaning "same" or "steady," is the process by which a system maintains a state or behavior stable enough, within limits acceptable to its structure, to survive. For the original text, consult Cannon's famous book *The Wisdom of the Body*. In the human body, blood-sugar levels, the amount of water in the blood, body temperature, blushing, shivering, and pupil dilation all change or increase when trying to keep something else in the body constant.

In another example of homeostasis, let's explore the often heard quote: "One bad apple ruins the whole lot." What does that mean? Chemically speaking, it means that once one apple starts to decay, the gas it releases provokes other apples to do the same. All the apples are trying to "get in synch."

In both the living and nonliving environments in our world, interacting units of matter, no matter what they are, tend toward equilibrium. We have *evolving* systems everywhere. In the most typical example, some species become extinct and others, very similar but with perhaps only a very small, almost indiscernible difference, live on. In a less typical example, the amazing reproductive relationships between specific flowers and specific insects *evolve* in such a way that makes them uniquely suited for survival in their habitats.

Teachers often fear using the word "evolution" due to the religious and political controversy it often sparks among adults. Antagonists of the theory most often attribute a unique value to human life on Earth, and that issue most often constitutes the center of the controversy. The evolution of humankind, however, is not a typical topic of formal study in preschool or primary school. It involves a number of concepts with little developmental relevance in the world of young children. However, if students ask questions about human evolution, the NSTA position statement on the teaching of evolution, found at www.nsta.org, provides a useful guide to how teachers can respectfully and professionally respond.

Concepts related to evolution, such as *change, balance,* and *equilibrium,* on the other hand, have tremendous conceptual importance in classrooms with young children. See Chapter 12, "Science in the Shopping Cart," for more specific details.

MAKE MODELS, COLLECT EVIDENCE, AND OFFER EXPLANATIONS

Earlier, we saw how children make sense of their world through the development of *models*. The key word is "development." Remember how some children used petroleum jelly to model how a polar bear's blubber insulates its internal body and how others used black construction paper to model how a polar bear's black skin absorbs heat from the sun. For other children, the jelly and the black construction paper were just that—jelly and construction paper, not models of blubber and skin. Teachers can guide children's thinking, not dictate it.

Models take many forms. They can help children and adults *explain* what we see happening, and are useful until proven incomplete or inaccurate. Models help scientists and engineers understand how things work; they can be physical items, diagrams, or equations. Children may use whirligig-type models to mimic how a seed pod falls to the ground. But they can also sketch a seedpod and use arrows to show the direction of the travel. Adults may use a set of equations that accounts for gravity, acceleration, and the other variables in the system. Although models can take many forms, teachers of young children must think of "model" as a verb, rather than as a noun. How can teachers help children create dynamic real models of the larger world in children's immediate world? They must use "real" material.

Use the Real Thing!

Ms. Penner may ask the children, "Do plants really need sunlight to live?" She can solicit their answers and reasoning, then guide them into a process whereby she asks, "How can we use real plants to show that what you are saying is true?" In Ms. Penner's mental plan, she may try to guide them into modeling the importance of the sun in plant growth by putting some plants in darkness and some in the sun and watching them over time. But she must work with the children's present conceptions of "a good plan" as her instructional starting point.

Ms. Penner must, whenever possible, use the genuine three-dimensional material that is being studied. For the unit on plants, she needs real seeds, soil, and water, and perhaps the "artificial sun" of a grow light.

Explain with Evidence

Evidence consists of data on which to base explanations. Scientific *explanations* incorporate existing and new evidence from observations, experiments, or models into the simplest statements possible. "Hypothesis," "model," "law," and "principle" are different terms to describe various types of scientific explanations.

Ms. Penner provides rich learning opportunities without using these terms but by inviting children to engage in the type of thinking from which explanations emerge.

"Jane, can you explain your problem to Leslie. She is working on something similar and you might be able to help each other."

"Let's listen to Jamal and carefully watch how his model works so that we'll be able to offer him the ideas he has asked us for."

MEASURE WHAT CHANGES AND WHAT STAYS CONSTANT

Everything in our world is in the process of *changing*. Yet these changes often serve to keep something *constant*. Let's look at how plants and animals and the environment interact.

Changes occur everywhere: Seedlings become trees; trees decompose. It all happens as a result of processes tempered with metabolic regulators to maintain homeostasis—in this case, a balance between photosynthesis and respiration. Changes in systems can be *measured*, and the measurement provides evidence of change and contributes to the formulation of new scientific explanations. There are different systems of *measurement* for different purposes, and deciding when to use which one is an important decision for the learner. Below is a unit on plant growth that incorporates the unifying science concepts just discussed.

PLANT GROWTH: A BIOLOGY UNIT

Seeds, which have stored food, can germinate in the dark—because they don't need light. When the food is used up, the sprouted seeds, called seedlings, need light. At this point, the seedlings need the sun as a source of energy. This energy is used to produce food through a process called photosynthesis.

The unifying concepts are described specifically in terms of this unit on plant growth, part of a larger study of living environments.

Big Ideas

What does Ms. Penner need to know about plants in order to successfully teach this unit? She first learns about the relationship among the forms of the various plant parts and the functions they perform.

- Plants have certain *forms*, chloroplasts, that *function* to produce glucose, food for the plant.
- Glucose is a *form* of stored energy for the plant.
- The process of the plant producing its own food also *functions* to produce oxygen.
- Plants *function* as sources of nutrients and oxygen for animals.

Ms. Penner looks at the role of plants in the systems of our Earth:

- Plants provide oxygen to the Earth's atmosphere, allowing animals that need oxygen to survive. Thus animal respiration and plant photosynthesis form an interactive *system*.
- Plant growth follows a predictable *order* (seed, seedling, mature plant, harvest, decomposition) and *organization* (releasing carbon dioxide, taking in water, etc.).

Ms. Penner examines the evolution of plants over time.

- Plants began as algae about 450 million years ago. As they *evolved* they developed adaptations. Some plants created a waxy cuticle in order to protect themselves from drying out. For example, a desert cactus retains water to help it survive long periods of drought and contains pricklers to protect itself from animals. Other plants developed a hard seed case that opens up under extreme conditions.

Ms. Penner models plant growth and searches for ways to collect reasonable evidence as part of her own professional preparation for the unit.

- *Models* of plant growth in highly acidic conditions can provide *evidence* of the effects of acid rain. This is an example of a *model* providing the *evidence* we seek to answer questions about emerging environmental concerns.
- What is the *evidence* that makes us think that what we know is true? In science, we test our ideas and collect enough *evidence* to confirm that our results are predictable. When the growing profile of plants in highly acidic conditions is replicated over and over again, we consider this *evidence* that acid rain is detrimental to the life cycle of the botanical world.

Ms. Penner thinks about the aspects of plant growth that can be measured.

- Plants *change* as they grow—in size and in appearance. For example, seeds slowly germinate. A soft stem with small green leaves grows from the ground. As it continues to grow the stem becomes longer and stronger and leaves spread out in order to receive more light. At the tip of the plant a bud will appear. At a certain point and time, the flower will open up and the petals, rich in color and fragrance, will catch the eye of animals that might help in its reproduction. It is possible to *measure* all aspects of plant growth: height, numbers of leaves, petals on flower, et cetera.

Problems of Emerging Relevance

Invite children to suggest a plan for "getting the seeds to start growing." Typically the children will want to put the seed in the ground and add water. Allow the children to do so but also encourage them to test it under different conditions. For example, Will the seed begin to grow without the soil? Or will the seed grow with water only? You might wonder aloud whether or not the seeds need light to grow. Depending on children's answers, encourage them to plant their seeds under different conditions.

Have available different-size paper, different types of writing instruments, digital cameras if possible, tape recorders if appropriate, and any other device or mechanism with which the children might record their observations and thoughts.

The initial problem of wanting to create the right conditions for growth of the children's chosen seeds gives rise to a number of other problems that emerge as relevant to the children. The teacher needs to be prepared to gather supplies and to foster the conditions about which the children wonder. Their wonderment typically meanders through type of soil, depth of the seed, the number of seeds in each hole, the amount of water, and a variety of other factors that they perceive as important.

Materials/Procedures

Have available the following supplies: many sizes of pots, cups, buckets, watering cans, and sprinklers; plastic wrap of different colors; soil; vermiculite; sand; pebbles; cheesecloth; and seeds of many varieties. If possible, gather both old and new seeds. If older seeds are not available, some teachers put a few seeds in a microwave oven for a few seconds. Doing such kills the seeds, and the seed will not germinate. The idea that not all seeds germinate, a viability issue, is an important one for children to consider as they think about not only their garden, but food production in general.

Have the materials visible, labeled, and readily available but, instead of distributing materials, encourage the children to choose the material best suited to their investigation.

Although food production and distribution are everyday natural occurrences on which we all depend, they are removed from the daily life of most adults and young children. Therefore, planting a vegetable garden is one way to bring young children closer to the science of food production and distribution on which their very lives depend.

The level and nature of engagement with the ideas of how food is produced and distributed depends on the developmental level of the children in the class. But generally, after the harvest when there are no more classroom green beans and peas, children have a reference point to appreciate the harvest cycle.

Assess Student Learning

As has been stated in previous chapters, teaching and assessment are flip sides of the same coin. The assessment tools that inform teaching are the same tools with which a teacher instructs. Careful listening to the children's hunches, asking children to explain their predictions, and requesting follow-up to children's original statements are all mechanisms by which the teacher assesses student learning and determines next teaching steps.

This chapter concludes Part 3, "From Unifying Science Concepts to Curriculum." We now turn to the final section of the book, Part 4, "From Curriculum to the Wonder of Science." Chapters 12 and 13 illustrate two challenge-based curriculum units that integrate reading, writing, listening, speaking, and drawing with science and math concepts and processes. Chapter 14 concludes the book with some important safety measures and approaches to creating viable learning spaces.

FROM CURRICULUM TO THE WONDER OF SCIENCE

Chapter 12

Science in the Shopping Cart: A Chemistry Unit

This chapter presents a unit within which children explore essential ideas about our world through mixing and matching ingredients and designing and developing their own products from items easily purchased in supermarkets and grocery stores. This unit prompts learning of the unifying concepts through problem-based investigations of chemistry concepts and processes.

There are five lessons, each of which asks young children to build ideas out of the evidence emerging from their activity within the lesson. The lessons prompt children to build concepts aimed at unifying what they already know with what they are learning from their current investigations.

Every lesson begins with a challenge situation used to intrigue children with the lesson's big ideas. The value of posing problems of emerging relevance has been discussed throughout the book, and this chapter offers five field-tested lessons with this type of open-ended yet specific problem of emerging relevance. Each lesson includes descriptions of the lesson's big ideas, materials, and procedures, and multiple ways to assess children's learning.

Clean-Up Time

This lesson invites children to explore the chemistry of substances through the challenge of creating a unique cleansing product to make tarnished pennies sparkle again. Upon creating their product, children figure out how to fit the three-dimensional shape holding their new product into a new three-dimensional shape they just built to package and sell their product.

Open-ended lessons include the potential for a number of big ideas, dependent upon how a teacher chooses to negotiate the lessons with children. Here are some big ideas that children can explore in this lesson, expressed in language designed for teacher background.

Big Ideas

A teacher's facility with assessing children's thinking is essential for the teaching of big ideas. Thus, descriptions of the big ideas and some sample ways of assessing children's interaction with and construction of those ideas are linked in this section. Some of the most common big ideas related to this lesson include:

- Proof in science requires the scientist to control variables.
- Matter exists in different phases.
- Different jobs require different tools.
- Some substances interact with each other and create new substances.

Most children of all ages begin with a mixing of multiple ingredients. Challenge children to pinpoint the most effective ingredients from their mix (but note that students younger than 5 or 6 years old rarely accept the challenge). Introduce or remind children of the "one change at a time" rule—that is, the children can change anything they wish, but encourage them to change only one thing at a time.

Ask early readers to look at the labels of the ingredients to see if they can spot any similar substances among them.

Encourage children to document their work in any format—notes, quantities used, diagrams, pictures, and so forth. Highlight the idea that to make another batch of their cleaning product or to improve it, they will need to know what is in it!

As children work on creating their own products, invite children to compare and contrast ingredients, analyze various materials for different uses, evaluate tools for efficiency and effectiveness, and design a system to determine the success of the products they produce. Take notes on their responses and activities. These responses are windows into their thinking.

The Science of Commercial Cleaners

Some cleaners use a mechanical rather than chemical method of cleaning. These are known as abrasives. Scouring powders and even toothpastes contain abrasive components. Salt is a great mechanical cleaner, although it also has a number of chemical cleaning abilities. Mechanical cleaners are good learning tools for young children because, to some degree, they can perceive what is happening as they scrub and rub. Chemical cleaners provide a plethora of phenomena for children to witness and about which to reason.

Commercial cleaners often contain acids—substances that add hydrogen ions (H^+) to a solution—or bases, substances that add hydroxyl ions (OH^-) to a solution. Bases are also known as alkalis. Some examples of acids are lemon juice, vinegar, and colas. Bases include products such as bleach, ammonia, and antacids.

Acids and bases react with each other and with other substances, sometimes very rapidly and violently. They break apart each other. Since most of the substances in our everyday life are more acidic than basic, bases are often used as cleaning agents. One way that children can classify substances as acids or bases is with the natural acid/base indicator red cabbage juice, which will change color dependent upon how strongly the substance is acidic or basic.

Solvents are liquids that can dissolve other substances. Water is often known as the universal solvent because it can dissolve an enormous variety of substances. Water will surround and break apart these substances. This is what occurs when we say something dissolves in water. Because water is a polar molecule (it has slight negative and positive charges on different atoms of the molecule), it can interact with other polar substances.

However, not all substances are polar substances; so water is not efficient in cleaning some substances. Waxes and oils are examples of nonpolar chemicals that require solvents other than water. They dissolve in products such as turpentine or acetone (nail polish remover)—neither of which is to be used with children. The information is included here for teacher background only.

Another way to clean waxes, oil, grease, and fats is with an interesting group of cleaners called detergents. Detergents are chemicals that have two different properties: they dissolve in water, which we learned is a polar substance, but they can also break apart fat and grease, which we learned are nonpolar substances. To clean these hard-to-clean, nonpolar substances such as fat and grease, manufacturers of laundry detergents have added enzymes, biological molecules that speed up the reactions of the detergents with the "dirty" substances to be cleaned away. In concentrated forms, detergents can irritate human skin and even the object that is being cleaned—so they should not be used with children. This information is only provided as background for teachers.

Problem of Emerging Relevance

Here is a cleaner that we can use to shine our dirty pennies. Can you improve the cleaner, and get our pennies to sparkle?

Make an environmentally friendly cleaner of water and chalk, and give that to the children as the "test" cleanser. Children may choose to improve the simple cleanser you have made, or they may choose their own materials and start from scratch.

Invite children to discuss what products they have seen at home. What cleanser is for what? What cleans wood? What cleans glass?

For children kindergarten age and older, their "purchasing" of ingredients with a bag of a predetermined number of beans sometimes changes the task from effusive "mixing" into a more deliberate approach to the product-creation process. It also extends the lesson into an authentic mathematics lesson involving counting, and the potential for other mathematical processes embedded in addition and subtraction. The lesson can also extend into the artistic realm with the following problem of designing an appealing package, naming it, and marketing it:

Let's sell your products in our classroom store. Each product will need a name and a package.

With this extension, children tackle the creative challenges of constructing a three-dimensional shape and experimenting with language as they sell their product, among many other endeavors.

Material/Procedures

vinegar	catsup	barbecue sauce	lemon juice
seltzer water	chalk	toothpaste	small cups with lids
sponges	toothbrushes	stirrers	mortar and pestle
paper	cardboard	tape	crayons
aprons	goggles	gloves	

Start by making the materials in the preceding list available in labeled, easy-access containers of small quantities and invite children to help solve the problem. A constraint in this problem is that there are no traditional brand-name cleaning products available.

As the children's thinking develops and as they share thoughts on how to proceed, secure other materials specific to the children's unfolding investigations.

Color without Crayons

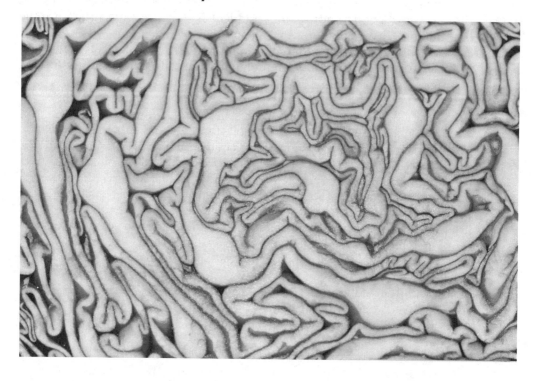

This lesson invites children to explore the fascinating world of indicators. Many natural dyes found in flowers, fruits, and vegetables make good indicators—substances that transform under certain conditions and serve as clues about the nature of other substances. Typically, the transformations are color changes. In this lesson, we use red cabbage juice, a substance that changes color dramatically in the presence of acids or bases, to "color without crayons."

Open-ended lessons include the potential for a number of big ideas, dependent upon how a teacher chooses to negotiate the lessons with children. Here are some big ideas that children can explore in this lesson, expressed in language designed for teacher background.

Big Ideas

A teacher's facility with assessing children's thinking is essential for the teaching of big ideas. Thus, descriptions of the big ideas and some sample ways of assessing children's interaction with and construction of those ideas are linked in this section. Some of the most common big ideas related to this lesson include:

- Proof in science requires the scientist to control one variable at a time.
- Quantities matter—measure!
- Order matters—keep track!

- Different jobs require different tools.
- Substances can be categorized by how they react in cabbage juice: some substances turn pink, others turn green, and still others do not change color at all.
- Boiling red cabbage extracts chemicals called anthocyanins, which are responsible for the color changes that occur when the red cabbage solution comes in contact with acidic or basic substances.

The color of any material is due to its chemical makeup, and it is this chemical makeup that determines how light reflects off of material and how our eyes see it. The specific color changes allow us to use red cabbage solution as an indicator of the presence of an acid or a base. Red cabbage solution turns from dark purple to bright pink in the presence of acids. This change occurs because acids change the chemical makeup of cabbage so that it reflects more red light waves. Red cabbage turns from dark purple to green in bases, which change the chemical makeup of cabbage so that it reflects more green light waves. In solutions that are neutral (neither acidic nor basic), red cabbage remains its original dark purple color.

Red cabbage is only one naturally occurring acid/base indicator. There are many other natural indicators—notably beets, cranberries, blueberries, hydrangeas, and geraniums. Some only work for acids; others only work for bases. Some children may want to design an experiment to prove that one or more of these new indicators can detect an acid or a base, or both or neither!

As children create and explore, encourage them to keep track of their findings in ways that are appropriate to them and their conclusions: drawings, sketches, photos, writing, and so on.

Problem of Emerging Relevance

The problem-based learning situation for this lesson is:

Let's put on a "Color Show" in our small cups! Can we turn some purple to pink, some purple to green, and then back to purple?

Material and Procedures

red cabbage	milk	orange juice
vinegar	grapefruit juice	cream of tartar
broccoli juice	seltzer water	saltwater
sugar water	paintbrushes	coffee filters
spoons	stirrers	1 oz. cups and lids
liquid droppers		

Have all of the above materials in labeled 1-ounce cups and an attached liquid dropper, with a supply of empty paper or plastic cups and liquid droppers available in quantities sufficient for the size of the whole group. Each child or small group will need several empty cups.

Encourage children to combine a few drops of cabbage juice and a few drops of their "test" solutions in an empty cup to see what color the cabbage juice turns, if it turns at all. Can they get pink cups to turn back into purple? What would they have to add? Encourage them to keep track of their work in the ways that suit them best.

Making a Red Cabbage Indicator

Cut a head of red cabbage into small pieces and boil it for about 10 minutes in as little water as is necessary to cover the cabbage. Slowly pour the solution into a jar and store it in the refrigerator. Portion it into small cups for the children's use, and make it available to children with liquid droppers for dispensing.

Make sure children wear aprons to protect their clothes and plastic gloves to protect their hands from the cabbage solution which, although edible and of course nontoxic, can stain fingers. Use nonlatex gloves, due to the prevalence of latex allergies. Although all the products are safe, everyday items, within the context of a science experiment, children should still wear goggles to protect their eyes in case of squirting from the liquid droppers or spills.

There is no tasting allowed in this experiment, so that any possible allergic reactions or the spreading of germs or contaminants can be avoided.

After the children have had multiple opportunities to experiment, present the following challenge. *How about drawing a picture of our color show using our special color show papers?*

To prepare color show papers, soak coffee filters in red cabbage juice and let them dry. Children can draw on these special papers using toothpicks, cotton swabs, or paintbrushes dipped in any of the substances with which they experimented. The color that emerges on the paper is determined by the product that they used as a "paint."

Shake It Up

This lesson invites children to separate "curds and whey" and "butter and buttermilk." In this lesson, children can develop a number of measurement skills: counting the number of shakes, tracking the hands of an analog clock, or watching the figures on a digital clock. They can also engage in reading or listening to nursery rhymes, and exploring legends and historical accounts of food production around the world. This lesson provides a setting within which children can study the historical development of ideas in science.

Open-ended lessons include the potential for a number of big ideas, dependent upon how a teacher chooses to negotiate the lessons with children. Here are some big ideas that children can explore in this lesson, expressed in language designed for teacher background.

Big Ideas

A teacher's facility with assessing children's thinking is essential for the teaching of big ideas. Thus, in this section, we link descriptions of the big ideas to examples of assessing children's interaction with and construction of those ideas. Some of the most common big ideas related to this lesson include:

- Milk is a complex substance.
- Butter can be made from the cream in milk.
- Cheese can be made from warm acidified milk.
- Acids play a role in making cheese.

- Salt can preserve foods.
- Science evolves through people's ideas.

How children go about handling the ingredients and their informal conversations as they proceed are windows into the nature of their thinking. Take notes on children's spontaneous talk. Encourage reasoning. For instance, if two children measure their quantities, inquire with them as to how their quantities differ. Are they smaller larger, heavier, lighter, longer, shorter, et cetera? Children's responses can help the teacher determine next steps in mathematics lessons, or possible groupings of children for follow-up investigations, or extensions for the current lesson that will address children's current ideas.

Problem of Emerging Relevance

The problem-based learning situation for this lesson is:

What happens when you mix one small cup of heavy cream and two small cups of milk in a clean jar with a lid and then shake the closed jar hard and steady? What do you get?

Focus children's attention on the appearance of the mixture. Ask them to remove the lid and periodically look inside as they shake. The two products emerging—curds and whey—are part of many children's diets, but today we refer to them as cottage cheese.

After making curds and whey, read the nursery rhymes "Little Miss Muffet" and "Betty Botter."

Little Miss Muffet

Little Miss Muffet sat on a tuffet,
Eating her curds and whey;
Along came a spider who sat down beside her
And frightened Miss Muffet away.

Betty Botter

Betty Botter
had some butter,
"But," she said,
"this butter's bitter.
If I bake
this bitter butter,
it would make
my batter bitter.
But a bit of
better butter—
that would make
my batter better."

So she bought
a bit of butter,
better than
her bitter butter,
and she baked it
in her batter,
and the batter
was not bitter.
So 'twas
better Betty Botter
bought a
bit of better butter.

Material/Procedures

heavy cream	milk	clean plastic jars with lids
measuring containers	cheesecloth	small cups
bread or crackers	nonsharp spreading utensils	small weights

Butter on the First Round

The children are invited to shake a jar of one part of heavy cream and two parts of milk. The instructions include the purposely ambiguous "small cups" phrase so that the children can use any first measure and then need to figure out how to double it for the second measure. The teacher makes available small cups in order to conserve materials and keep costs low. When the children see the solids in their jars, ask them to skim off the solid. That's the butter. The liquid is the buttermilk.

Cheese on the Second Round

The children heat the buttermilk in a safe manner, placing it near a sunny window or immersing it in a tub of hot water. After it has warmed up a bit, have them pour in a few drops of vinegar or lemon juice and let it sit for 1 hour. Let them pour the mixture through cheesecloth to separate the chunky curds from the liquid whey. This will be a challenge for them and there will be spills. Model problem-solving behavior by having paper towels nearby and, if possible, some extra curds and whey that you have previously made. Let the curds drip off any remaining buttermilk by hanging them for a little while in the cheesecloth. You now have soft cheese in the cheesecloth.

Have safety goggles available and a helping adult to supervise a bucket of hot water or some heat source.

Cream separates in the shaking jar into a solid (butter) and a liquid (buttermilk). Spread the solid over a piece of bread, or gluten-free crackers for those with wheat allergies, and with parental permission the children can taste the fresh butter.

Milk, when heated and with the aid of some coagulant (in this case, an acid), separates out into solids left on top of the cheesecloth (curds) and liquid that strains through the cloth (whey). Spread the solid over a piece of bread or any food item to which the children have no allergies, and with parental permission the children can taste the solid. It is soft cheese.

Interested children can continue the process by washing the butter and preserving it through salting in the style of the 18th-century farmer. Mix in 1 spoonful of salt for every 2 cups of butter. Before use, farmers would wash out the salt. Cheeses were also salted for preservation.

Have scales available for children to find the mass of the various ingredients before and after their procedures. Guide appropriate use of the scale and computations.

Sticking Together

This lesson provides children with a simple plan for making glue, a plan without amounts of ingredients indicated. Children test different measures of ingredients to make a glue that works—which successfully keeps a paper chain together. Children experiment with methods of filtering, heating, and cooling. Making glue from cow's milk always surprises the children. Making waterproof glue from milk, which is mostly water, surprises the adults!

Open-ended lessons include the potential for a number of big ideas, dependent upon how a teacher chooses to negotiate the lessons with children. Here are some big ideas that children can explore in this lesson, expressed in language designed for teacher background.

Big Ideas

A teacher's facility with assessing children's thinking is essential for the teaching of big ideas. Thus, descriptions of the big ideas and some sample ways of assessing children's interaction with and construction of those ideas are linked in this section. Some of the most common big ideas related to this lesson include:

- Matter is characterized by different attributes.
- Different ratios of substances produce different textures and consistencies.
- The order in which substances are mixed, heated, or cooled influences their behaviors.
- Temperature affects how substances combine or separate.
- Different jobs require different tools.
- Water can change the characteristics of a substance.
- Science evolves through people's ideas.

Foster note-taking in whatever form is appropriate to the needs and abilities of the children. Some children will be able to write independently, some can take digital photos, and some will draw pictures. If you or another adult can scribe for the children as they dictate to you, this process fosters the scientific process and is an important dimension of early writing development. Introduce (or remind children of) the "one change at a time rule," discussed earlier in the chapter. Their responses are indicators of the variables they presently consider as they engage in the task. Take note of how individual children respond. In the process of making glue, help children measure, document what they are doing, and share their reasons for what they are doing. For instance, the procedure says "warm the milk." How do the children try to warm the milk? If they decide to submerge the milk in hot water, how do they manipulate the container of milk? There are multiple decisions to be made for every step of the procedure, and how children make decisions is a window into their thinking. Take note of their procedures.

Problem of Emerging Relevance

The problem-based learning situation for this lesson is:

We're hoping to create a paper chain for the school festival. Let's make some glue to keep the paper links together. Here is the recipe for making glue:

- Warm the milk, add vinegar, and stir.
- Design a method to separate the curds and whey.
- Add baking soda and water to the curd.
- You have glue. If not, change the measures of ingredients.

Show the children labels of various white glues. They usually have a picture of a cow on them. Ask the children what that might mean? White glues are usually made from milk.

Show children the following recipe. Quantities are purposely not listed in the procedure to encourage dialogue and comparisons and learning from children who begin earlier than others. The recipe, written in this manner, engages children in thinking about what they are doing and in problem solving along the way. All ingredients are dispensed and measured in small quantities.

Material/Procedures

milk	cold water	hot water
coffee filter paper	sieves	cheesecloth
vinegar	baking soda	orange juice
lime juice	lemon juice	3" x 12" paper strips
1 or 2 oz. cups	stirrers of any type	

Have safety goggles available and a helping adult to supervise a bucket of hot water or some heat source. As an extension of this lesson, powdered milk or milks of various fat contents (skim, 1%, or 2%) can be added as experimental variables.

If this lesson follows the "Clean-up Time" lesson, you might want to use the cabbage juice again as an indicator for the presence of acids or bases. Encourage the children to test the milk and the vinegar.

Bring in stories about the inventiveness of our ancestors in the various uses of milk products. For instance, the history of cheese, ice cream, and resin plastic are fascinating stories for youngsters of all ages.

Cover with Crackers

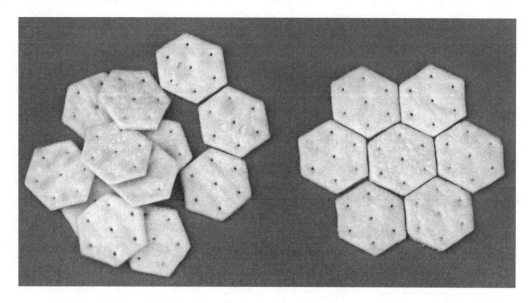

In this lesson, children begin an exploration of tessellations by trying to completely cover a rectangle with crackers of various shapes. What are tessellations? The word refers to pictures or designs composed of shapes that repeat to cover the surface of a plane in a symmetrical way with no overlapping or gaps, as seen in the above picture. The word *tessera* in Latin means "a small stone cube." The cubes were used to make *tessellata*, mosaic pictures commonly found in Roman buildings. Tessellation can also be called *tilings*.

In this lesson, children try to translate their 3-D design to a drawing on paper. Children extend their study by considering the role of tessellation in ancient art and current design, as well as the advantage of using tessellation design in making crackers. Open-ended lessons include the potential for a number of big ideas, dependent upon how a teacher chooses to negotiate the lessons with children. Here are some big ideas that children can explore in this lesson, expressed in language designed for teacher background.

Big Ideas

To teach big ideas, a teacher must have facility with assessing children's thinking. In this section, we link descriptions of the big ideas and examples of ways of assessing children's interaction with and construction of those ideas. Some of the most common big ideas related to this lesson include:

- Tessellations can be made by rotation (to rotate an object means to turn it at some angle) or reflection (to reflect an object means to produce its mirror image) or translation (to translate an object means to move it, but not turn it or put it in its mirror image).
- Some regular shapes tessellate with themselves. Examples are triangles, squares, and hexagons.

- Some regular shapes tessellate with each other. Examples are octagons and squares, hexagons and triangles, dodecagons and triangle, dodecagons, squares, and hexagons.

Translating the design of the crackers onto paper, a 3D-to-2D challenge, is difficult not only for young children, but also for adults. Some children enjoy the challenge and spend a considerable time drawing. Other students begin free-form drawing that is not directly tied to the tessellation challenge.

As children work, use the conventional terms for polygons, but do not correct children when they use their own terms for each shape. Encourage children to use the terms "mirror image" when thinking about reflection, "gliding" when thinking about translation of shapes, and "turning" when thinking about rotation. All of these concepts lie at the core of geometry and form the foundations of chemistry.

When we offer young children opportunities to build conceptual foundations of reflections, rotations, and translations as they apply to crackers on a rectangle, we also offer them possibilities to better understand molecular interactions on a microscopic level in the future.

Problem of Emerging Relevance

The problem-based learning situation for this lesson is:

In how many ways can we completely cover this rectangle with the crackers, with no crackers on top of each other and no spaces between crackers?

Material/Procedures

assorted crackers	assorted ceramic tiles	assorted wooden shapes
markers	pencils	crayons
scissors	graph paper	blank paper
dot paper	rectangles, approx. 12" x 12"	small mirrors

Note: Make available various crackers that tessellate, and a few that do not. Also, have available crackers that tessellate with each other.

Web Resources

http://gwydir.demon.co.uk/jo/tess/grids.htm#dotri
http://mathforum.org/library/topics/sym_tess
http://www.tessellations.org/index.htm
http://www.mcescher.com

M. C. Escher is the most well-known artist to have used tessellations in his art. Download a few prints from the resource links above for use with children.

The next chapter reinforces the lesson-planning ideas presented in this chapter with another curriculum model using a different topic: water.

Chapter 13

Water, Soil, Sand, and Salt: An Earth Science Unit

This chapter focuses on the unique role played by water on our planet and in our lives, along with the fascinating interactions among water, soil, sand, and salt. What follows is a unit of problem-based investigations of physical science concepts and processes, also including opportunities for children to study properties of water, sand, soil, and salt in relationship to the biology and chemistry phenomena of our planet.

Each of the five field-tested lessons invites teachers and children to work together to address a variety of ageless and timeless challenges through observing, exploring, and engaging in some type of transformation, either taking something apart or putting something together. In each lesson, teachers intentionally highlight the combinations and reconstructions emerging from the children's actions and statements and invite young children to link their prior experiences with their findings from their activities.

Using the same lesson structure of Chapter 12, every lesson begins with a challenge situation used to intrigue children with the lesson's big ideas and includes descriptions of the big ideas of each lesson, materials and procedures, and multiple ways to assess children's learning.

At Water's Edge

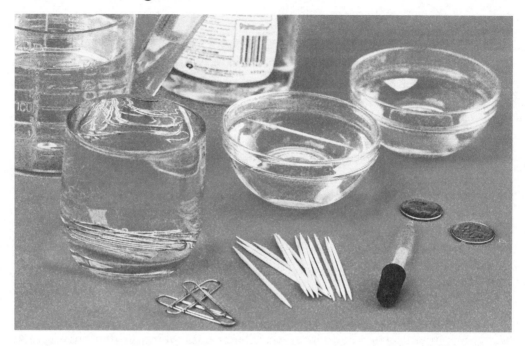

This lesson consists of four directed activities that give rise to a number of others the children typically suggest themselves. Children are fascinated by the remarkable characteristics of water and the role water plays on our planet and in our lives. From the highly domed shape of water droplets to insects being able to walk on ponds, water's many amazing properties and wide range of phenomena make it a topic in which children have immediate interest and through which children can better understand our planet.

Young children need not use the term "surface tension." Yet surface tension and its highly cohesive forces are what explain many of water's powerful properties. In this lesson, children observe shape, size, and number; practice fine and gross motor skills as they pour, place, grip, and squeeze; produce transformations in surface tension; and classify characteristics of pure water versus soapy water.

Open-ended lessons include the potential for a number of big ideas, depending upon how a teacher chooses to negotiate the lessons with children. Here are some big ideas that children can explore in this lesson, expressed in language designed for teacher background.

Big Ideas

A teacher's facility with assessing children's thinking is essential for the teaching of big ideas. Thus, descriptions of the big ideas and some sample ways of assessing children's interaction with and construction of those ideas are linked in this section. Some of the most common big ideas related to this lesson include:

- Water has a high surface tension and cohesive forces.
- Soap or detergent breaks water's surface tension.
- Pure water can dome above a cup; soapy water cannot.

As has been stated in previous chapters, teaching and assessment are different aspects of the same activity. The assessment tools that inform teaching are the same tools with which a teacher instructs. Carefully listening to the children's guesses or reasons, asking children to explain their predictions, and requesting follow-up to children's original statements are all mechanisms by which the teacher assesses learning and determines next teaching steps. For instance, a teacher might show pictures of water striders—insects that can walk on water—and ask the children to compare the insect on the water to the experiments they have just performed.

The quests described in the next section—mound up water on a quarter, pile up paper clips in a cup of water, get boats to scoot across a homemade bay, or force toothpicks to move away from each other in a bowl—all create the "need to know" and offer opportunities to think about properties of water. While the children are working, ask them to share their hunches about what is going on and encourage them to keep track of their ideas in any way that seems fitting to the child's age and proclivities. Do they want to write, draw, photograph, dictate, sketch, or sculpt?

Problem of Emerging Relevance

This lesson includes four activities that look different, but which explore the same concept—namely, that water has high surface tension and cohesive forces keeping it together.

Task 1. Does your cup run over?
- Fill a glass with as much water as it will hold.
- How many paper cups can you add to the full glass of water?
- Observe the surface of the water.

Task 2. How many drops can George hold?
- Predict how many drops of water you can put on a quarter before the water rolls off. Try it again.
- Add a drop of detergent to the water on the coin. What happens?

Task 3. Can your boat scoot around?
- Cut a flat boat shape from an index card. Float the boat in water. Place one drop of detergent behind the boat. What happens? Try it again.

Task 4. Toothpicks and water
- Gently place two toothpicks on the surface of the water in a bowl. Place one drop of detergent between the two toothpicks. What happens?

Materials

small easy-to-pour containers with water	liquid droppers (plastic pipettes)
small nonbreakable dishes	index cards or wax paper or thin cardboard
toothpicks	scissors
many paper clips	small clear plastic cups

TEACHER NOTES

To continue the students' investigation of the surface tension of water and its changing properties in the presence of soap or detergent, offer children new questions that emerge from their tasks. For example, if children ask if a quarter will hold fewer drops of dirty water than clean water, encourage them to try it out. Help them make dirty water by adding soils and grasses, perhaps, to clean water, and help them count and compare water drops.

Squeaky-Clean Water

This lesson presents a very simple-sounding task—cleaning dirty water—but one that is filled with opportunities to construct an experiment, learn about controlling variables, gauge time, compute distance, determine particle size, sequence a series of activities and, in general, address a host of science-processing skills.

Cleaning dirty water incorporates conservation principles and holds an enormously important role in all community life. This lesson can illustrate the necessity for team work and creative thinking in a neighborhood in order to assure that we have clean water to drink and use.

Open-ended lessons include the potential for a number of big ideas, dependent upon how a teacher chooses to negotiate the lessons with children. Here are some big ideas that children can explore in this lesson, expressed in language designed for teacher background.

Big Ideas

A teacher's facility with assessing children's thinking is essential for teaching big ideas. Thus, descriptions of the big ideas and some sample ways of assessing children's interaction with and construction of those ideas are linked in this section. Some of the most common big ideas related to this lesson include:

- Filtration can separate solutes from solvents and large solutes from small solutes.
- The size of the filter matters in what task it can accomplish.
- Smaller pore size can slow down the purifying process, but can make it more effective.
- Loss of water occurs while trying to clean it.

Children can tell you much about their thinking through their actions. Document the children's sequence of events, question-posing, hunches, and/or statements of reasons as assessment of their learning.

Talk with children about how to approach the problem and discuss what materials need to be assembled. From this discussion, you can infer much about the children's prior conceptions. The teacher should monitor for safety.

Separation techniques abound in the science community as a common experimental tool for finding out how our world works. Focus children's attention on different ways to filter. Encourage attention to them describing the nature of the solutes; particle sizes; the pore sizes of the sieves, strainers, fabrics; and so on.

Since accomplishing the task requires multiple steps and observations of incremental change, many teachers use this activity to focus on scientific processing and writing skills.

Problem of Emerging Relevance

Filter the dirty water until you are satisfied with its cleanliness. Use any material, tools, or design you think will work.

Material/Procedures

water	soil, salt, sand, pebbles, and other safe local materials
paper towels	coffee filter paper
cheesecloth	mesh
strainers	funnels of different sizes
colanders	cups and buckets of different sizes
goggles	dissecting microscope or pocket microscope
magnifying glasses	clear tubing of different diameters and lengths
aprons	various colored papers as background
gloves	sieves with different pore sizes

Many children are attracted to the dissecting microscope. Be sure to have available different colored papers as backgrounds on which to view the various soil "contaminants."

Most children will not think about timing the procedures. After several untimed endeavors, use this lesson as an opportunity to discuss the potential value of timing: Do communities want to purify their water in the shortest period of time?

Fruits in a Flood

This lesson uses fruit to explore concepts of sinking and floating within the larger framework that all objects in our world are part of larger systems. Fruit provides a readily available source of small dense objects and large less-dense objects that help children question how objects behave in water. The lesson uses the power of children's transforming sinkers into floaters and floaters into sinkers to address concepts of "stuff" and "space."

In this lesson, teachers refer to the matter an object consists of as "stuff," and the volume that the matter takes up as "space." The lesson engages children for long periods because their investigation gives rise to many splinter questions: Does a fruit's floating or sinking change over time on its own? Does peeling the fruit change anything? Does cutting the fruit matter? Adding salt changes the floating. Does sugar change it? And the questions continue.

Open-ended lessons include the potential for a number of big ideas, dependent upon how a teacher chooses to negotiate the lessons with children. Here are some big ideas that children can explore in this lesson, expressed in language designed for teacher background.

Big Ideas

A teacher's facility with assessing children's thinking is essential for the teaching of big ideas. Thus, descriptions of the big ideas and some sample ways of assessing children's interaction with and construction of those ideas are linked in this section. Some of the most common big ideas related to this lesson include:

- Objects are more buoyant in saltwater than in fresh water.
- An object can float in one solution but not another.
- Whether or not an object floats is affected by the solution.
- Certain peeled and unpeeled fruit behave differently in water.
  (Peeled oranges sink in water. Unpeeled oranges float in water.)

The process of suspending a piece of fruit directly in the middle of a cup of water is a difficult task. But it is a task that is worth the effort. The process of adding salt, then adding water, and then doing both again is the equivalent of balancing an algebraic equation and is, thus, an important activity that can serve as a referent for mathematics to come.

Engage the children in articulating their reasons. Focus their attention on how much orange peel there is, or invite them to separately float the peel and the pulp. The terms "rind" and "skin" are also often used for the covering of the orange. Some students actually separate the thin orange peel from the white bitter pericarp, known as "pith," to show that that is not the peel but the pith, or "white stuff" that floats.

The teacher needs to actively listen to children as they engage in interaction with the fruit and water and foster new questions that extend the children's inquiries. Use the activity time to take notes on student conversations and musings. They are sharing their hypotheses and their views on salient variables. The teacher can document this information on student thinking for future discussion.

Problem of Emerging Relevance

Handing each child a cup of water with a grape sitting on the bottom, the teacher presents the following problem-based learning situation:

Here is a grape in a lake. Can you make the lake into a salty ocean and get the grape to swim underwater right in the middle of the ocean?

Allow the children to spend time on the problem. During and after suspending their grapes, encourage them to talk about their findings and share their reasoning. Respond with other challenges appropriate to the children's investigations.

In a follow-up challenge, show the children a big bucket of water and a whole orange. Ask them what they think will happen when the orange drops in the big bucket of water. After the children share responses, put the orange and the big bucket of water aside without dropping in the orange. Instead, hand out small bowls of water and orange slices, cross-sectional slices with the peel, and suggest:

Experiment with these slices, then tell your classmates if you want to change your mind about your prediction about the whole orange in the big bucket.

Some students will peel their orange slices, which has a dramatic effect on its buoyancy. Some will return to the grape and peel it, drop it in the water, and notice little effect on its buoyancy.

Materials/Procedures

clear plastic cups	small spoons
grapes, white and red	oranges, whole and sliced
other fruit, as available	
water in containers from which children can independently pour	
salt in containers from which children can independently scoop	
sugar in containers from which children can independently scoop	

When using any food item in an inquiry, it is important that the teacher model and highlight respectful handling of these natural products that provide nutrition for the world's population.

This inquiry can prompt children to think about fruit, in general, and can lead to other lessons that investigate fruits unique to settings around the world. When engaging in this inquiry, children often start investigating the property of buoyancy with a variety of non-food items.

Waterwheels at Work

In this lesson, children explore principles of engineering as they design waterwheels and refine them to make them work. In order for the waterwheel to do the work of lifting cargo, children need to design ways to put together three different pieces of the "puzzle" so that all of the pieces move at the same time. The children create systems to make a wheel, a shaft, and a cup of pennies move together! It's a challenging task, but one that inspires spontaneous applause by all when it is accomplished.

Some children can design a working waterwheel from scratch. Some children with spatial organization that is less developed will need to see a few waterwheels already set up, either purchased or made by other children, in order to begin the lesson as an exploration of the sort of work that the waterwheel can do. The engineering challenge for children who cannot make a waterwheel but who can use a waterwheel is to move cargo up and down, which they generally want to repeat many times. Dry rice, as an alternate to water, can also be used with purchased waterwheels to engage children in explorations of forces (see picture below).

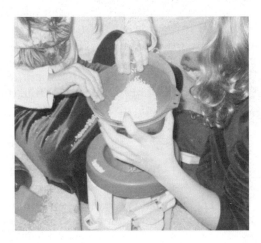

Open-ended lessons include the potential for a number of big ideas, dependent upon how a teacher chooses to negotiate the lessons with children. Here are some big ideas that children can explore in this lesson, expressed in language that is designed for teacher background.

Big Ideas

A teacher's facility with assessing children's thinking is essential for the teaching of big ideas. Thus, descriptions of the big ideas and some sample ways of assessing children's interaction with and construction of those ideas are linked in this section. Some of the most common big ideas related to this lesson include:

- The wheel and shaft is a machine.
- The shaft is the rod that goes through the wheel and turns it.

- Machines can change the direction of a force.
- Machines use energy for work.
- Power is the amount of work done in a certain time.

Waterwheels have been used throughout history as a means of using the power from a flow of water. One of the most common uses of waterwheels has been to mill flour in gristmills, but waterwheels have been and are used to power boats on rivers and calm waters and to power factories of all types.

There are many types and variations of waterwheels, but essentially they all consists of some type of wheel, either vertical or horizontal, with blades or buckets on a rim that catch the water and push the wheel. The wheel is connected to a shaft that, in turn, is connected to something to do some type of work: light a bulb, grind grain, or lift cargo, among many other tasks.

There are two main types of wheels. Overshot wheels catch a stream of elevated water, such as a waterfall, and undershot wheels typically catch water from the bottom of the wheel, as in a moving river or stream.

The principles of engineering in designing a waterwheel are fundamental principles involved in all human-made machines and include the same cycle of trials and improvement. A common "first try" produces a wheel that moves and a shaft that doesn't. Recognizing that the shaft is not moving is one important milestone; designing a way to get the shaft to move with the wheel is another. Adding a cup of pennies to the waterwheel–shaft combination is yet another big challenge. While the children work, teachers take notes, offer engineering advice, and co-explore with the children.

Problem of Emerging Relevance

The problem-based learning situation for this lesson is:

HELP WANTED!! We need a waterwheel engineer. Design your ultimate wheel to lift one cup of pennies from the dock to the deck!!!

To prepare the learning space, use a big cardboard box that has been notched at the top. Rest a small wooden dowel on the notches to serve as a shaft for the wheel. You also can also use two chairs with a dowel resting on the tops of the chairs and secured with tape or boards, as shown in the following picture.

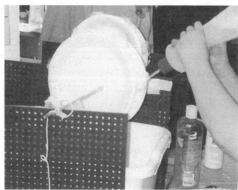

Material/Procedures

masking tape	scissors
paper clips	pennies, as cargo
string	squeeze bottles filled with water
paper towels and cloth towels	mop
1- or 2-oz. cups to serve as paddles	1- or 2-oz. cup lids to serve as paddles
dowels or cardboard tubes to serve as wheel shafts	
supports for wheel shafts under which a large pan can fit	
large aluminum foil "roasting pans" to catch the water	
Styrofoam plates to connect and serve as wheels	
waterproof glue for attaching wheels, cups, and lids	

Aiming squeeze bottles of water at different locations on the waterwheel changes the lift power. Children can explore the differences of aiming water at different parts of the waterwheel.

Teachers can be ready with suggestions to jump-start the design process. For instance, a teacher might suggest that children attach a cup of pennies to the shaft by taping the string to the shaft and taping the other end to the cup. With that prompt, children typically take the idea and adapt it to their own thinking.

Sand from Shore and Store

Sand is generically considered "loose particles of hard broken rock." But this definition doesn't capture the joy it brings to young children and really people of all ages. Sand has a number of uses. It is an ingredient in bricks and concrete, it is used to purify water and sandblast buildings, it can be oiled and used as molds in sand casting, it can be glued to paper and used for making wood smooth, and—what surprises children most—it is the principle ingredient in glass.

This lesson provides structured opportunities for children to take a closer look at these amazing grains of time to piece together stories about their world through sifting, sorting, and separating them, then combining them in new ways.

Open-ended lessons include the potential for a number of big ideas, dependent upon how a teacher chooses to negotiate the lessons with children. Here are some big ideas that children can explore in this lesson, expressed in language that is designed for teacher background.

Big Ideas

A teacher's facility with assessing children's thinking is essential for teaching big ideas. Thus, descriptions of the big ideas and some sample ways of assessing children's interaction with and construction of those ideas are linked in this section. Some of the most common big ideas related to this lesson include:

- Sand has different characteristic when it is wet and dry.
- The same volume of sand can look different in different containers.
- Sand consists of differently sized and shaped particles.

Children at different ages use sand to meet different needs and reach different milestones. Toddlers often use sand to explore their senses. They like to feel the sand in various ways. They may put it in their mouth, at which point the teacher can briefly say, "Sand is for playing, not eating."

Next, children like to build with sand, either going up, making towers and building, or going down, making tunnels and caves. By age 4, most enjoy dramatic play and use the sand to make their imaginative worlds and the items in it. Sand can become a cake and a cup of juice to pretend to eat and drink, or it can become a bracelet molded on the wrist.

What is sand? The composition of sand is largely dependent on where it originates. The sand on many beaches in Hawaii is made up of glass and minerals from volcanic rock fragments. On California's beaches, sand is largely quartz, with maybe some feldspar and other minerals from nearby mountain ranges. The sand in areas not near volcanoes or mountains may be almost entirely shell fragments or coral or animal skeletons. By looking closely at grains of sand, their size, texture, and color, we can try to interpret where it may have been, for how long, and maybe where it is heading.

This lesson provides an opportunity for children and the teacher to write to friends and relatives from different geographical areas asking for some sand from their area. It becomes an authentic letter-writing activity, with the delight of receiving a package in the mail sometime later. Sand from different areas contains different elements, thus looking and behaving differently. Sand with iron in it absorbs heat rapidly; therefore, making a trip to the water's edge on a hot day can burn your feet. Sand with limestone, on the contrary, is cool to the touch.

Dependent on the type of sand being investigated, this lesson can venture into many other scientific topics. If the iron content is high, use the lesson to study magnetic forces. Give the children magnets and see if they can pull the iron filings from the sand. Or place the sand on a coffee filter and put a magnet under the filter. The children might be able to see patterns due to the magnetic field. Although playing in the sand may be a typical childhood event, and even though we fortify breakfast cereals with iron, have the children wear gloves.

The International Sand Collectors Society has been studying sand for many years. It has compiled much information and can send you sand samples. Visit www.sandcollectors.org/Sand_Discoverx.html/.

The sand lesson is rich in language arts opportunities. Use appropriate terminology: pour, mold, tunnel, funnel, bridge, sift, sort, categorize, separate, transform, test, prove, empty, full, slope, deep, shallow, wide, narrow, absorb, wash, heavy, wet, crumble, turn, share, ask, tell, plan, pound, pat, and shape.

Problems of Emerging Relevance

"Manufacture" a bucket of "earth" for each child or small group. The bucket of earth can contain the following dry ingredients: finely sifted sand, course sand, rocks, stones, gravel, shells, pebbles, clay, marbles, buttons, beads, and a few surprise items that are unique to each bucket.

The problem-based learning situation for this lesson is:

Here is a bucket of earth. Sort it into as many different items as you can find. Show your friends. Then use your items to make your own artwork.

As the children go about their process of creating, differentiate the task for children at varying development stages. If you have children in your class who desire less-structured molding or pouring activities, direct them toward the sterilized sand with water and containers of varying shapes. Or, for a more directed activity, present the following challenge:

Here is a timer. You have two minutes and one red bucket. How many red buckets of sand can you bail from this tub to the tray?

With buckets that differ in volume by whole numbers—that is, a bucket and one that is twice or three times its volume—present the following:

How many red buckets does it take to fill one blue bucket? How many blues to fill one white? Is there a pattern?

Older or more advanced children may benefit from the dynamic model offered by pouring beads into a tall, narrow clear acrylic tube and analyzing the layering patterns. The process of beads layering in a tube is similar to how sand separates. Have various-sized beads of different colors available.

Drop the beads into the tube and watch how the tube fills. Try the task again in a new tube with new beads, but drop them in a different order. Is there a difference?

Material/Procedures

sterilized play sand	sieves
unfiltered sand from outdoors (lake, garden, ocean, etc.)	sifters
beads of at least three different sizes	strainers
narrow, tall clear acrylic tubes with one end capped	mesh
cups to hold sand, rocks, and gravel	cheesecloth
ladles with handles at different angles and different lengths	coffee filters
differently shaped containers for molding and comparing volumes	spoons
natural items (shells, wood, river stones) with smooth edges	magnets
dissecting/pocket microscopes	magnifying glasses
small nonlatex gloves	

For beautiful images of an artist's work, mostly with sand, using materials and tools found on any shore, go to www.protozone.net/jarnow/beachworks.html. There you will find a series of photos of Al Jarnow's "cities by the sea."

Learning with sand can get messy. Make keeping a tidy classroom part of the learning. Store the following clean-up materials nearby, in view, and labeled: a long-handled, flat broom, a dustpan and brush, and a whisk broom.

As this chapter and Chapter 12 illustrate, a teacher plays a multitasking role in a classroom based on constructivist learning principles. In the next chapter, the concluding chapter of this book, we explore the features of how a teacher sets up learning spaces to engage children in scientific thinking.

Chapter 14

Putting It All Together

So much of young children's growth and development is predicated on types of thinking that are scientific. Yet historically, organizing early childhood settings for the explicit teaching of science has been secondary to the focus on mathematics, art, and literacy. This chapter concludes the book by offering strategies for creating environments that are conducive to rich science experiences that also foster growth and development of skills and knowledge across the disciplines.

THE CLASSROOM AS LABORATORY

How a teacher prepares classroom space sets the stage for the type of learning that can occur there. There exists a range of factors that contribute to the successful design of a learning space. Wien, Coates, Keating, and Bigelow (2005) suggest that teachers consider elements such as:

- How do children use the various areas of the classroom?
- What makes the inviting areas of the class inviting?
- Where do negative behaviors occur, and why might they occur there?
- How does the room look from the height of a child?

Answers to these questions can guide teachers in the arrangement of furniture, centers, supplies, opportunities, and other dimensions of classroom life.

Researchers need a laboratory in which to conduct their research. For children, their "lab" must be outfitted with an abundance of materials that can be used in multiple ways. Children need access to information (either through books, the Internet, or other means) and the ability to acquire materials that become relevant as their investigations progress. A teacher providing opportunities for children to request materials honors her students' points of view, extends their investigations to the leading edge of their thinking, and allows the learning space to become a real laboratory.

A "real" laboratory does not require expensive or complicated equipment. As a new teacher once remarked, "I'm surprised to learn that you can do much with so little." Science materials for young children's experimentation need not be more than everyday objects, often the items we toss in recycle bins or common substances found in a kitchen or office.

Accessibility of Materials

Once acquired (ordered, donated, or purchased), materials must be accessible in a number of ways. It is important for children to be able to see the materials, rather than having them hidden in a closet or cabinet. In this way, children can choose the materials specific to their investigations. Baskets made from natural materials provide a low-cost, lightweight means of organizing.

The teacher plays an important role in deciding how and when to bring out specific materials and how and where to place them in order to prompt student thinking. If children are pouring rice from one bucket or beaker to another, the teacher can quietly place funnels with different-size openings or strainers of different-size mesh nearby. This small teacher action can prompt decidedly new pathways for investigation of matter, movement, forces, and more. The funnels may have been visually present in another nearby basket, but the nonverbal, subtle placement of the different funnels within reach of the child's present experimentation open up new avenues of thinking.

The word "can" in the above sentence is important to highlight. The new funnels and strainers might prompt new pathways of investigation. Or they might not. A teacher must be careful not to thrust upon a child something *the child* does not think she needs. Materials provide intellectual opportunities, but only if the child sees the opportunity in the material.

Organization of Materials

Teachers must organize materials in ways that expand rather than limit children's thinking. The organizational structure of materials must permit children's ideas and questions to flourish through their experimenting with the materials, so that the children can invent ways to use the materials to solve problems and think in multiple ways—including art, dance, music, and storytelling, among many others. For instance, a shelf labeled "vessels to hold things" may include everything from beakers to zippered bags to boxes, prompting children to decide what type of container would work for their needs. What attributes of the container are important for the task at hand (flexible, transparent, airtight, flat bottomed, et cetera)?

Similarly, a box labeled "tools to measure" may house the spring scales, thermometers, and rulers, enabling students to think of measurement broadly and in very divergent domains. With this organizational structure, children and teachers have the chance to talk about and "pass up" a thermometer as a tool to measure "hotness" if they are looking for the coiled-up tape measure as a tool to measure the length of a long, straight object.

Children begin to organize their thinking about investigations, while the organization of the materials helps them investigate.

The Necessity of Water!

Every learning center for young children requires readily available access to water, and the technology to heat it or cool it. Water is an essential ingredient in our daily lives and is also the major substance on Earth and in our bodies. Water is a substance with unique properties that allow life as we know it to exist on our planet. Pure water is a safe substance that provides numerous learning opportunities for people of all ages, but particularly for those of young ages. Having a sink with running water is an ideal. However, if that is not possible, the teacher can use tubs, jugs, buckets, bins, and thermoses.

Safety

Safety during science explorations must always be a first priority. Proper safety may look different between the home and the school. In classrooms, teachers must always follow school policies and state and federal regulations to ensure student safety. In this section we will talk about how to use common materials in a safe manner to maximize learning and minimize the likelihood of a child being hurt.

- *Eyes*: The word "chemical" conjures up images of toxicity, hazards, and danger; however, everything around us is a chemical of some sort: orange juice, milk, and even water. When making pasta in your home, you would not typically wear goggles to boil the water, but in a formal learning environment, you would. When mixing chemicals in your home—for instance, cocoa powder and warm milk—you wouldn't think of putting on goggles, either. However, in a formal learning center, you would. Why? We use goggles to protect the children's eyes and our own because sometimes even safe items can become dangerous if mixed. Picture baking soda and vinegar trapped in a bottle with a cork and think of the danger to the eyes that the cork poses once it becomes a projectile.
- *Nose*: We can use the early childhood science experience to begin teaching the basic protocols of research. How do we whiff something in a science research lab? We put the container containing the substance in front of our nose and use one hand to gently waft the fumes toward us. We teach children never to put their face directly over the container.
- *Mouth*: In early childhood science experiences, tasting new foods, comparing tastes of known foods or preparing a dish to eat is common. We need to teach our young children that when we research foods in this manner, it is acceptable to taste them. However, most experiments do not involve putting anything in one's mouth. Children need careful instruction not to put anything from a learning environment into their mouths without adult permission. It is imperative that learning centers for young children have a reference instrument handy to test all objects that could become a choking hazard. A choke tube is a small cylinder with an opening the size of a child's mouth or stretched esophagus. Any ball, toy piece, or object children may handle must be larger than the opening of the choke tube.
- *Hands*: Changing the temperature of items to see what happens, learning to measure in degrees, or preparing an ingredient for a meal

are important learning activities but must be handled with appropriate safety measures. Students must wash their hands before and after handling materials and must protect their hands with appropriate insulation when touching anything potentially very cold or very hot. Teachers must instruct students not to try any experiments at home without the permission of their parent or caregiver. This is especially true when students are working on electricity, magnetism, and light and sound studies.

To prevent cuts and abrasions, use plasticware instead of glassware whenever possible. Have materials readily available to clean up spills and breakages, and be sure to have a classroom protocol in place when spills or breakages occur. When using thermometers, be sure to use new ones that are filled with alcohol rather than old ones that are filled with mercury.

- *Feet*: Children must not transport items that are heavy or are of a shape that, if dropped, could injure their feet. Wearing closed-toed shoes is also advised if liquids are being transported or explored.

NSTA Position Statements

The National Science Teachers Association (NSTA) provides national and international leadership in science education. It distributes free of charge— as well as posts on its Web site—a number of position statements on critical issues that are important to the teaching and learning of science. Be sure to consult the following guidelines by logging on to www.nsta.org.

- Responsible Use of Live Animals and Dissection in the Science Classroom
- Students with Disabilities
- Elementary School Science, Environmental Education
- Gender Equity in Science Education
- Use of the Metric System
- Multicultural Science Education
- Parent Involvement in Science Education
- Safety and School Science Education

"VERBS" FOR LEARNING SCIENCE

All the carefully acquired and well-organized materials in a room with plenty of water and a stove and refrigerator are not sufficient to create a learning environment that is conducive to the construction of knowledge. The learning environment needs to be brought to life, and it is the pedagogical vision of teachers that determines how energetic and intellectually nurturing the setting can become.

We now present a series of fundamental early childhood activities— things to do, or "verbs"—to review the major ideas of the book.

Young Researchers Sort and Separate

Separating things that work together to better understand each part are fundamental research activities. Today, in biochemistry research labs all over the world, scientists use a jelly made from seaweed and an electric current to separate big pieces of DNA from little pieces of DNA in order to determine its origin. Likewise, children can use strainers and colanders to sift rocky soil or cheesecloth and coffee filters to get clear water. Children might also use the strainers and colander for the dirty water and the cheesecloth and coffee filters for the rocky soil. The children decide what tools are best for what purpose.

They then sort through their own experimental data. A young child will likely not say, "The pore size in the coffee filter is too small to separate the rocky soil." But a child may say: "The circles on the colander are too big to catch the pieces of dirt in the water." The teacher may wonder out loud why no soil came through the filter and may suggest looking at it with a pocket microscope. The teacher narrates the child's world and offers vocabulary as new words become a shorthand for concepts the child is building.

Young Researchers Test and Transform

Indeed, children learn a lot from watching. But in terms of understanding transformations, they learn more from making them than watching them. Children need learning opportunities to ask themselves, "How can I make it change?"

What is the difference between puzzlements that can lead to understanding and mysteries that remain magical? The difference lies in the level to which children can contribute to unraveling the puzzlement. If children can change something and observe the outcomes of the changes they make, the likelihood of their learning increases.

Children can engage in two types of transformations: combinations and reconstructions.

- Combinations involve rearranging parts, such as blocks, figurines, or doll clothes and include concepts and terms such as fewer, greater, or different.
- Reconstructions involve changing substances, such as water, sand, or clay and include concepts and terms such as more, less, or different.

In order for a child to transform something, the child must design what to do and how to do it, which is a level of ownership that focuses the mind on the outcomes of actions.

Young Researchers Mix and Match

Mixing and matching are vital activities that allow today's scientific research community to add new knowledge to public conversations about our world. Research laboratories produce new products from the synthesis of materials that had not been linked previously, or the use of materials used in new ways. Likewise, in classrooms and at home, children can create their own recipes to make various items—for example, hand lotions, juice drinks, or pasta products—and develop proficiency in measuring, ordering, and computing, among other basic skills.

The human brain mixes and matches phonemes as it reads text, equal values as it solves math problems, and tops and bottoms to get its body dressed in the morning. Combining objects and ideas is a mental activity in all types of human behavior and interaction.

We can look at a good conversation as a combination of utterances through which the speakers make meaning. Providing opportunities for young children to mix and match with a purpose is not only part of a good science curriculum, it is part of a nurturing and engaging environment, in general.

Young Researchers Design and Develop

Today's scientific research laboratories spend a great deal of time and effort designing and developing new products, protocols, and procedures. Water bottles, for example, are redesigned to use less plastic in an effort to produce less non-biodegradable refuse. The water in the bottle is purified in new ways or enhanced with new additives in an effort to increase sales. The water is bottled using new procedures to cut down on costs or distributed from plants that use new energy sources in order to pay less tax.

Similarly, children can engage in the same type of systems thinking on which the adult world operates, but within a domain and in a nature appropriate to children's lived experiences. Designing and developing products and procedures are challenges that children find exciting and challenges through which they share their unfolding talents.

LESSON PLAN MODEL

The following lesson plan model can be used to design a unit of study ranging from 1 day to many weeks. It provided the template for all of the lesson plans and unit plans throughout this book.

Big Ideas

Write a user-friendly explanation of the science topic. Include specific examples and enough detail so that you can effectively facilitate children's engagement and respond to their questions.

- How do the science concepts fit into the children's everyday lives?
- What are the unifying science concepts you will highlight?

Assessment: Discuss how you might adjust the big idea to respond to students' different understandings. What are the precursor concepts and what are the advanced concepts?

Problems of Emerging Relevance

- What is the "problem" or challenge for the students to solve?
- Describe how you will organize the lesson. What will students do

in this lesson that will promote the learning of the subject matter? What extensions might you have for early finishers?

Assessment: Discuss how you might change the problem for different students in your class.

Materials/Procedures

Discuss the materials you and your students will use for the lesson and what the students might do with the materials to carry out their investigations of the problem. Describe the safety issues.

Assessment: Discuss how you might change the materials and procedures for different students in your class. Think about ways that your students can extend their thinking in related domains. Provide Web sites, literature, and other resources that can enhance student thinking in different ways.

Assess Student Learning

- How will you help children discuss what they have learned or the questions they have generated?
- What qualities will you foster in student work, and how is your assessment connected to the lesson objectives and standards you target?
- How will you help students organize and structure their learning?
- What assessment tools will you use to inform your teaching?
- How will you establish checkpoints within the lesson to determine student understanding?

BECOMING A PROFESSIONAL

The *National Science Education Standards* (National Research Council, 1996), referenced thoughtout this volume, is a document that emerged as the result of the nation's goal that all students achieve scientific literacy in order to appreciate their role as citizens in our changing times. The precursor to these standards is the *Benchmarks for Scientific Literacy* (American Association for the Advancement of Science, 1993). These two documents synthesize the work of many commissions, councils, panels, and committees of thousands of scientists and educators.

Also highly visible on the present educational scene is the No Child Left Behind Act (NCLB), authorized in 2001, which includes numerous policy mandates. The standards and the mandates, however, often evoke conflicting legislative and administrative directives to teachers and schools.

CONFLICTING MESSAGES

Teachers today face a number of challenges with conflicting messages. Whereas the Science Standards advocate a more problem-based, student-centered approach to science learning, many federal and state mandates emphasize standardized testing and punitive funding measures when schools do not meet testing benchmarks.

The Science Standards view curriculum as a process, a process in which teachers select strategies based on the best available understandings of how children learn. Curriculum in response to policy mandates, however, often involve factual recall of information published with pacing schedules instructing the teacher when to be at which place in the curriculum.

The Science Standards emphasize child-generated inquiry and transferable skills that are appropriate to the child and the learning situation at hand. Policy mandates, on the contrary, often seek curriculum delivered precisely and concisely and on time. Although these mixed messages exist, a thoughtful teacher can employ strategies that help children learn skills that prepare them for success on standardized tests. Children's disciplined wonder under the guidance of a good teacher results in conceptual knowledge built from thinking about evidence . . . and that measures up very well on tests.

The National Research Council presents countless studies indicating that meaningful education requires teacher judgment based on assessment of student understanding (Donovan & Bransford, 2005). Simply stated, in order for a teacher to maintain an intellectually rich, meaningful educational environment for young children, the teacher must co-investigate with the children and allow them to teach her how to teach them.

NAEYC's (2009) final standard, "Becoming a Professional," concludes this book with the notion that professional educators put children's welfare and education at the center of their practice and engage in the types of professional learning that continually lead them to greater insights regarding how to accomplish the goal.

Becoming a Professional

Candidates identify and conduct themselves as members of the early childhood profession. They know and use ethical guidelines and other professional standards related to early childhood practice. They are continuous, collaborative learners who demonstrate knowledgeable, reflective, and critical perspectives on their work, making informed decisions that integrate knowledge from a variety of sources. They are informed advocates for sound educational practices and policies.

Perhaps the wisdom of a dear sailing friend, Captain Demosthenes Pagonis, sums up how teachers of young children might think about creating spaces for learning: "You can't trim the wind. You can only trim the sails" (Pagonis, personal communication, May 7, 2009).

A SIMPLE MESSAGE

This book began with a simple message and ends with the same one: explore with the young people in your life the splendid surprises new days bring, and you'll be a science learner and a science teacher all in one!

References

Abbott, M. L., & Fouts, J. T. (2003). *Constructivist teaching and student achievement: The results of a school level classroom observation study in Washington.* Seattle, WA: Washington Research Center, Seattle Pacific University.

Adler, M. (1940). *How to read a book.* New York: Simon & Schuster.

American Association for the Advancement of Science. (1993). *Benchmarks for science literacy.* New York: Oxford University Press.

Andrews, G., Halford, G. S., Bunch, K. M., Bowden, D., & Jones, T. (2003). Theory of mind and relational complexity. *Child Development, 74*(5), 1476–1499.

Astington, J. (1993). *The child's discovery of the mind.* Cambridge, MA: Harvard University Press.

Astington, J. W., & Baird, J. A. (Eds.). (2005). *Why language matters for theory of mind.* New York: Oxford University Press.

Bereiter, C., & Scardamalia, M. (1989). Intentional learning as a goal of instruction. In L. B. Resnick (Ed.), *Knowing, learning and instruction: Essays in honour of Robert Glaser* (pp. 283–305). Hillsdale, NJ: Lawrence Erlbaum.

Bransford, J. D., Brown, A. L., & Cocking, R. R. (Eds.). (1999). *How people learn: Brain, mind, experience, and school.* Washington, DC: National Academies Press.

Brooks, J. G. (2002) Schooling for life: Reclaiming the essence of learning. Alexandria, VA: Association for Supervision and Curriculum Development.

Brooks, J. G., & Brooks, M. (1999). *In search of understanding: The case for constructivist classrooms.* Alexandria, VA: Association for Supervision and Curriculum Development.

Brooks, J. G., Libresco, A. S., & Plonczak, I. (2007, June). Spaces of liberty: Battling the new soft bigotry of NCLB. *Phi Delta Kappan, 88*(10), 749–756.

Brooks, J. G., & Thompson, E . G. (2005, September). Social justice in the classroom. *Educational Leadership, 63*(1), 48–52.

Carson, R . (1962). *Silent spring.* Boston: Houghton-Mifflin.

Carson, R. (1998). *The sense of wonder.* New York: Harper & Row. (Original work published 1956)

Center for Applied Special Technology (CAST). (2011). National Center for Universal Design for Living. Retrieved on January 17, 2011, from www.udlcenter.org/

Chalufour, I., & Worth, K. (2005). *Exploring water with young children.* St. Paul, MN: Redleaf Press.

Charles, C. (2009). Children and Nature Network. Retrieved February 8, 2011, from http://www.childrenandnature.org/research/

Charteris, J. (2010). *Time to go.* London: Paperlink limited.

Confrey, J. (1990). What constructivism implies for teaching. In R. B. Davis, C. A. Maher, & N. Noddings (Eds.), Constructivist views of the teaching and learning of mathematics. *Journal for Research in Mathematics Education,* Monograph No. 44 (pp. 107–124). Reston, VA: National Council of Teachers of Mathematics.

Confrey, J., & Kazak, S. (2006). A thirty-year reflection on constructivism in mathematics education in PME. In A. Gutiérrez & P. Boero (Eds.), *Handbook of research on the psychology of mathematics education: Past, present and future* (pp. 305–345). Rotterdam, Netherlands: Sense Publishers.

Cook, R. E., Tessier, A., & Klein M. D. (2007). *Adapting early childhood curricula for children with special needs.* New York: Prentice-Hall.

Damasio, A. R. (1994). *Descartes' error: Emotion, reason, and the human brain.* New York: Putnam.

Damasio, A. R. (1999). *The feeling of what happens: Body and emotion in the making of consciousness.* New York: Harcourt.

Damasio, A. R. (2003). *Looking for Spinoza: Joy, sorrow, and the feeling brain.* New York: Harcourt.

De Vries, H., & Goudsblom, J. (Eds.). (2002). *Mappae mundi—Humans and their habitats in a socio-ecological perspective: Myths, maps, methods and models.* Amsterdam: Amsterdam University Press.

Donovan, M. S., & Bransford, J. D. (Eds.). (2005). *How students learn: History, mathematics and science in the classroom.* Washington, DC: National Academies Press.

Duckworth. E. (1996). *The having of wonderful ideas.* New York: Teachers College Press.

Elkind, D. (1967). Egocentrism in adolescence. *Child Development, 138*(4), 1025–1034.

Faber Taylor, A., Kuo, F. E., & Sullivan, W. C. (2001). Coping with ADD: The surprising connection to green play settings. *Environment and Behavior, 33*(1), 54–77.

Fensham, P. (1992). Science and technology. In P. W. Jackson (Ed.), *Handbook of research on curriculum: A Project of the American Educational Research Association.* New York: Macmillan.

Forman, G., & Fyfe, B. (1998). *Negotiated learning through design, documentation and discourse.* Stamford, CT: Ablex Publishing Co.

Forman, G., & Hall, E. (2005, Fall). Wondering with children: The importance of observation in early education. *Early Childhood Research and Practice, 7*(2). Retrieved January 10, 2011, from http://ecrp.uiuc.edu/v7n2/forman.html

Forman, G., Hall, E., & Berglund, K. (2001, September). The power of ordinary moments. Retrieved January 10, 2011, from http://eclkc.ohs.acf.hhs.gov/hslc/ecdh/eecd/Domains%20of%20Child%20Development/Science/ThePowerofOrdi.htm

Forman, G., & Hill, F. (1980). *Constructive play: Applying Piaget in the preschool.* Monterey, CA: Brooks/Cole.

Fosnot, C. T. (2005). *Constructivism: Theories, perspective, and practice* (2nd ed.). New York: Teachers College Press.

Fromberg, D. P. (2009, April). How nonlinear systems inform meaning and early education. *Nonlinear Dynamics, Psychology and Life Sciences, 14*(1), 47–68.

Fuller, F. (1969). Concerns of teachers: A developmental conceptualization. *American Educational Research Journal, 6*(2), 207–226.

Furth, H. B., & Wachs, H. (1975). *Thinking goes to school: Piaget's theory in practice.* New York: Oxford University.

Goleman, D. (2006). *Social intelligence: The new science of human relationships.* New York: Bantam Books.

Gopnic, A., Meltzoff, A., & Kuhl, P. (1999). *The scientist in the crib: What early learning tells us about the mind.* New York: HarperCollins.

Gordon, D. T., Gravel, J. W., & Schifter, L. A. (2009). *A policy reader in universal design for learning* (pp. 5–18) Cambridge, MA: Harvard Education Press.

Hale, C. M., & Tager-Flusberg, H. (2005). Social communication in children with autism: The relationship between theory of mind and discourse development. *Autism, 9*(2), 157–178.

Hapgood, S., & Palinscar, A. S. (2007, December-January). Where literacy and science intersect. *Educational Leadership, 64*(4), 56–60.

Hesse, K. (1999). *Come on, rain.* New York: Scholastic Press.

Huttenlocher, P. R. (2002). *Neural plasticity: The effects of environment on the development of the neocortex.* Cambridge, MA: Harvard University Press.

Inhelder, B., & Piaget, J. (1958). *The growth of logical thinking from childhood to adolescence.* New York: Basic Books.

Kamii, C., & DeVries, R. (1993). *Physical knowledge in preschool education.* New York: Teachers College Press.

Kandel, E. R. (2007). *In search of memory: The emergence of new science of mind.* New York: Norton.

Kozol, J. (2005, September 1). Still separate, still unequal: America's educational apartheid. *Harper's Magazine, 311*(1864).

Krakovsky, M. (2005). Dubious "Mozart effect" remains music to many Americans' ears. *Stanford Report.* Retrieved January 5, 2011, from http://news-service.stanford.edu/news/2005/february2/mozart-020205.html

Kuhn, D. (1989). Children and adults as intuitive scientists. *Psychological Review, 96*(4), 674–689.

Lilley, I. M. (2010). *Friedrich Froebel: A selection from his writings.* New York: Cambridge University Press.

Linn, M. C., Davis, E. A., & Bell, P. (Eds.). (2004). *Internet environments for science education.* Mahwah, NJ: Lawrence Erlbaum.

Locker, T. (1997). *Water dance.* San Diego, CA: Hartcourt Brace.

Louv, R. (2008). *Last child in the woods: Saving our children from nature deficit disorder.* Chapel Hill, NC: Algonquin.

Louv, R. (January 7, 2010). Last child in the woods of pandora. Retrieved February 8, 2011, from http://www.childrenandnature.org/blog/2010/01/07/last-child-in-the-woods-of-pandora/

Malaguzzi, L. (1993a). For an education based on relationships. *Young Children, 49*(1), 9–12.

Malaguzzi, L. (1993b). History, ideas, and basic philosophy. In C. Edwards, L. Gandini, & G. Forman (Eds.), *The hundred languages of children: The Reggio Emilia approach to early childhood education* (pp. 41–89). Norwood, NJ: Ablex.

Marshall, E. (n.d.) Current brain research: What does it tell us and what does it mean? Retrieved on January 4, 2009, from www.state.gov/m/a/os/41189.htm

Matthews, M. (1998). *Constructivism in science education: A philosophical examination.* Norwell, MA: Kluwer.

Michaels, S., Shouse, A. W., & Schweingruber, H. A. (2007). *Ready, set, science! Putting research to work in K-8 science classrooms.* Washington, DC: National Academies Press.

Mitchell, L. S. (1916). A credo for Bank Street College. Retrieved on February 25, 2007, from www.bankstreet.edu/aboutbsc/credo.html

Moore, R. (1999). Healing gardens for children. In C. C. Marcus & M. Barnes (Eds.), *Healing gardens: Therapeutic benefits and design recommendations.* New York: Wiley.

Moore, R., & Wong, H. (1997). *Natural learning: The life history of an environmental schoolyard.* Berkeley, CA: MIG Communications.

National Arbor Day Foundation. (2007). *Learning with nature idea book: Creating nurturing outdoor spaces for children* (V. Cuppens, Ed.). St. Paul, MN: Redleaf Press.

National Association for the Education of Young Children. (July 2009). NAEYC Standards for Early Childhood Professional Preparation Program. Retrieved on January 16, 2011, http://www.naeyc.org/files/naeyc/file/positions/ProfPrepStandards09.pdf

National Association of Elementary School Principals and Educational Research Services. (2009, Winter). Research Round Up. Retrieved on January 9, 2011, from www.naesp.org/resources/2/Research_Roundup/2009/RR2008v25n2a3.pdf.

National Research Council. (1996). *National science education standards.* Washington, DC: National Academies Press.

National Research Council. (2000). *How people learn: Brain, mind, experience, and school.* Washington, DC: National Academies Press.

National Scientific Council on the Developing Child. (2007). *The science of early childhood development: Closing the gap between what we know and what we do.* Retrieved on November 29, 2010, from http://developingchild.harvard.edu/library/reports_and_working_papers/science_of_early_childhood_development

National Wildlife Federation. (2011). *Garden for wildlife.* Retrieved January 16, 2011, from www.nwf.org/gardenforwildlife/certify.cfm?campaignid=WH10A150

Naylor, S., & Keogh, B. (2000). Concept cartoons in science education. Sandboch, UK: Millgate House.

Nelson, C., & Luciana, M., (Ed.) (2001). *Handbook of Developmental Cognitive Neuroscience*. Cambridge, MA: The MIT Press.

Pagonis, D. (May 7, 2009). Personal communication.

Perkins, D. N., & Salomon, G. (1990). The science and art of transfer. Retrieved November 15, 2009, from http://learnweb.harvard.edu/alps/thinking/docs/trancost.htm

Perneger, T. V. (2006). Borges on classification. *International Journal for Quality in Health Care, 18*(4), 264–265.

Piaget, J. (1932). *The moral judgment of the child*. New York: Free Press.

Piaget, J. (1937). *The construction of reality in the child*. London: Routledge Classics.

Piaget, J. (1947). *The psychology of intelligence*. New York: Routledge Classics.

Piaget, J. (1965). *Insights and illusions of philosophy*. London: Routledge & Kegan Paul.

Piaget, J. (1981). *Intelligence and affectivity: Their relationship during child development*. Palo Alto, CA: Annual Reviews.

Pinker, S. (1999). *How the mind works*. New York: Norton.

Pinker, S. (2007). *The stuff of thought: Language as a window into human nature*. New York: Viking.

Premak, D., & Woodruff, G. (1978). Does the chimpanzee have a theory of mind? *Behavioral and Brain Sciences, 1*(4), 515–526.

Pugh, K. J., & Bergin, D. A. (2005). The effect of schooling on students' out-of-school experience. *Educational Researcher, 34*(9), 15–23.

Rose, D. H., & Vue, G. (2010). 2020's learning landscape: A retrospective on dyslexia. *International Dyslexia Association, Perspectives on Language and Literacy, 36*(1), 33–37.

Rutherford, F. J. (1991). Vital connections: Children, books, and science. In W. Saul & S. A. Jagusch (Eds.), *Vital connections: Children, science, and books* (pp. 21–30). Washington, DC: Library of Congress.

Sagan, C. (1995). *The demon-haunted world: Science as a candle in the dark*. New York: Random House.

Sheldon, K. M., & Biddle, B. (1998). Standards, accountability, and school reform: Perils and pitfalls. *Teachers College Record, 100*(1), 164–180.

Shonkoff, J. P., & Phillips, D. A. (Eds.). (2000). From neurons to neighborhoods: The science of early childhood development (Committee on Integrating the Science of Early Childhood Development; National Research Council; Institute of Medicine). Washington, DC: National Academy Press.

Shreeve, J. (2005). Beyond the brain. *National Geographic*. March, 2–31. Retrieved on Jan 5, 2010, from http://science.nationalgeographic.com/science/health-and-human-body/human-body/mind-brain.html

Siegel, D. J. (1999). *The developing mind: Toward a neurobiology of interpersonal experience*. New York: Guilford Press.

Siegel, D. J. (2001). *The developing mind: How relationships and the brain interact to shape who we are*. New York: Guilford Press.

Siegel, D. J. (2010). *Mindsight: The new science of personal transformation*. New York: Bantam Books.

Spock, B. (2004). *Preschoolers: Magical and egocentric thinking*. Retrieved on February 23, 2007, from www.drspock.com/article/0,1510,3901,00.html

Thompson, R. A. (2008, December). Connecting neurons, concepts, and people: Brain development and its implications. Preschool Policy Brief. *National Institute for Early Education Research, 17*.

Tirabosco, T. (2001). *At the same time*. San Diego, CA: Kane/Miller.

Tortora, G., & Grabowski, S. (1996). *Principles of anatomy and physiology* (8th ed.). New York: HarperCollins College.

Trefil, J. S. (2008). *Why science?* New York: Teachers College Press.

von Glasersfeld, E. (1995). *Radical constructivism: A way of knowing and learning.* London: Falmer.

Wadsworth, B. (1989). *Piaget's theory of cognitive and affective development* (4th ed.). White Plains, NY: Longman.

Warren, B., & Rosebery, A. S. (1992, August). Science education as a sense-making practice: Implications for assessment. In *Focus on Evaluation and Measurement* (Vol. 2), Proceedings of the National Research Symposium on Limited English Proficient Student Issues, Washington, DC, September 4–6, 1991. Washington, DC: U.S. Department of Education, Office of Bilingual Education and Minority Languages Affairs.

Wellman, H., Cross, D., & Watson, J. (2001). Meta-analysis of theory-of-mind development: The truth about false belief. *Child Development, 72*(3), 665–684.

Wien, C. A., Coates, A., Keating, B-L., & Bigelow, B. C. (2005). Designing the environment to build connection to place. *Young Children, 60*(3).

Wimmer, H., & Perner, J. (1983). Beliefs about beliefs: Representation and constraining function of wrong beliefs in young children's understanding of deception. *Cognition, 13*(1), 103–128.

Worth, K. (1998). The power of children's thinking. In *Foundations: A Monograph for Professionals in Science, Mathematics, and Technology Education, Vol. 2, Inquiry: Thoughts, Views, and Strategies for the K–5 Classroom.* Division of Elementary, Secondary, and Informal Education Directorate for Education and Human Resources. Washington, DC: National Science Foundation.

Worth, K., & Grollman, S. (2003). *Worms, shadows and whirlpools: Science in the early childhood classroom.* New York: Heinemann.

Yager, R. E., & Enger, S. K. (Eds.). (2006). *Exemplary science in grades preK-4: Standards-based success stories.* Arlington, VA: National Science Teachers Association.

Yoon, J., & Onchwari, J. A. (2006, June). Teaching young children science: Three key points. *Early Childhood Education Journal, 33*(6), 419–423.

Index

About the Author

Jacqueline Grennon Brooks is professor in the Department of Teaching, Literacy and Leadership, School of Education, Health and Human Services, Hofstra University, where she also serves as director of the Institute for the Development of Education in the Advanced Sciences and director of the secondary science education program. She is author of *Schooling for Life: Reclaiming the Essence of Learning* and coauthor with Martin G. Brooks of *In Search of Understanding: The Case for the Constructivist Classroom.*